THE ULTIMATE
BASKETBALL
TRIVIA BOOK

THE ULTIMATE
BASKETBALL
TRIVIA BOOK
600 QUESTIONS
FOR THE SUPER-FAN

SAM AMICO

SPORTS
PUBLISHING

Sports Publishing books may be purchased in bulk at special discounts for sales promotion, corporate gifts, fund-raising, or educational purposes. Special editions can also be created to specifications. For details, contact the Special Sales Department, Sports Publishing, 307 West 36th Street, 11th Floor, New York, NY 10018 or sportspubbooks@skyhorsepublishing.com.

Sports Publishing® is a registered trademark of Skyhorse Publishing, Inc.®, a Delaware corporation.

Visit our website at www.sportspubbooks.com.

10 9 8 7 6 5 4 3

Library of Congress Cataloging-in-Publication Data is available on file.

Cover design by Tom Lau
Cover photographs: Getty Images

Print ISBN: 978-1-68358-308-0
Ebook ISBN: 978-1-68358-309-7

Printed in the United States of America

To Katie, Brady, James, and Reece. We make quite a starting five.

Contents

Pregame

Believe it or not, basketball existed long before LeBron James. It existed before Kobe Bryant. It even existed before Michael Jordan, Magic Johnson, and Larry Bird—still the holy trinity of hoops in the eyes of many. In fact, basketball has been around so long that most of the NBA's founding fathers have passed on, leaving behind a shot clock, three-point line, All-Star Game, and other elements of the game that remain in place today.

The purpose of this book isn't solely to see how much you know. It's to celebrate a sport that has become rich in tradition, gone totally global and continues to grow.

It's to prove that the game survived just fine—even thrived—before the era of social media. It's to show that true centers used to count for something, that three-pointers were once only taken in times of desperation (as opposed to the central theme of the offense), that there was a time where defense was more than just a rumor, unless, of course, you played in the ABA.

Ah, yes. The old American Basketball Association. It was running and gunning and having tons of fun. It was fashion and flair, high-flying dunks and long-range bombs. It was dance teams, wacky halftime acts, crazy uniforms, loud music blaring throughout the arena, manufactured noise, and basically anything to let the fans get close and feel as if they were part of the action.

Sound familiar?

Of course it does. The ABA may have folded, but the NBA didn't really take off until it adopted many of its antics. Namely, the Association decided to start speeding up the game and selling its individual stars—often more than the teams themselves. It made every night an event, a rock concert that featured really tall men in baggy shorts and high tops, orchestrating a practically flawless ballet with a basketball. The game, no doubt, became more than a game. It became a happening.

But that doesn't mean what took place before all the hype was meaningless. At one time, both the pro and college games were little more than a good place to go if you were looking for a fight. Then, once the players quit fighting, they would trade their attempts to score some buckets by getting together to throw back some beers. Some of them even lit up in the locker room at halftime. Most of the pros had other jobs. These were the game's pioneers, people who played for a few bucks and for little other reason than to satisfy a passion. They wanted to build something that could survive. It seemed they never dreamed it could thrive. At least, most never envisioned it becoming the multi-billion-dollar industry it is today.

So, the pages that follow aren't intended only to test your knowledge, but also to entertain and inform. They are to honor the men and women who made basketball work, who poured their blood, sweat, and tears into shaping the game and those who are doing their part to keep it alive today.

Mostly, this book is for you. The fan. You may be the biggest part of the game. After all, without people who are willing to spend their hard-earned money to buy merchandise and watch, basketball doesn't survive. How big of a fan are you? The answer will most certainly lie in the questions that follow.

This is your NBA Finals, your Final Four, your chance to show how much you actually know.

As Bird said to Magic in the famous 1980s Converse commercial featuring the two legends in a game of one-on-one, "OK, Magic. Show me what ya got."

FIRST QUARTER

HISTORY

QUESTIONS

How did the NBA come about? Perhaps a little differently than you might expect.

The league was formed in 1946, when a bunch of hockey owners got together and looked for another way to help fill their arenas. They didn't know much about basketball, but a pro league sounded like a decent idea, so they went with that. Next thing you know, a bunch of hockey owners were now basketball owners.

That's basically the short version of why the NBA exists today.

But like any start-up, the league suffered through some growing pains. Unlike any start-up that still exists, the NBA's growing pains lasted about 35 to 40 years . . . or at least until Magic Johnson and Larry Bird came along. Then came Michael Jordan. Then Kobe Bryant and LeBron James and Stephen Curry, and the other great players of today.

Today, pro basketball has become one of the world's most globally adored sports and the NBA a league that is rich and tradition and history.

Question is, how much do you really know about that history? More than a hockey fan?

Hey, there's only one way to find out. Good luck in the pages that follow.

1. Who was the inventor of the game of basketball (called "Basket Ball") and how many original rules were written by the game's founder?
   Answer on page 11.

2. Who came up with the idea for a 24-second shot clock in the NBA?
   Answer on page 12.

3. In what season was the 24-second shot clock introduced?
   Answer on page 12.

4. What is the diameter of a basketball rim?
   Answer on page 12.

5. What type of ball was used for basketball when the game was first played?
   Answer on page 13.

6. Which arena hosted the first official NBA game?
   Answer on page 13.

7. Who is credited with being the pioneer of the jump shot?
   Answer on page 13.

So, how's your ABA knowledge?

8. Which team was *not* originally a member of the American Basketball Association?
   A. Dallas Mavericks
   B. San Antonio Spurs
   C. Brooklyn Nets
   D. Indiana Pacers
   Answer on page 13.

9. Who is the all-time leading scorer in ABA history?
   A. Billy Cunningham
   B. Artis Gilmore
   C. Dave Robisch
   D. Dave Twardzik
   Answer on page 13.

10. Who is the all-time leading rebounder in ABA history?
    A. Billy Cunningham
    B. Artis Gilmore
    C. Dave Robisch
    D. Dave Twardzik
    Answer on page 13.

11. Who is the all-time assist leader in ABA history?
    A. Billy Cunningham
    B. Artis Gilmore
    C. Dave Robisch
    D. Dave Twardzik
    Answer on page 13.

12. Who played in the most games in ABA history?
    A. Billy Cunningham
    B. Artis Gilmore
    C. Dave Robisch
    D. Dave Twardzik
    Answer on page 13.

13. Which ABA team reached an agreement—in perpetuity—to receive a portion of the NBA's television revenue at the ABA-NBA merger, but did not merge?
    A. Kentucky Colonels
    B. Virginia Squires
    C. Spirits of St. Louis
    D. Oakland Oaks
    Answer on page 13.

14. Only two players played in the ABA from the moment it tipped off in 1967 until it merged with the NBA and closed its doors in 1976. Can you name them?
    Answer on page 13.

15. Can you name the four teams that joined the NBA from the ABA in 1976?
Answer on page 14.

16. True or False. The longest game of the NBA's shot-clock era took place between the Detroit Pistons and Denver Nuggets in 1983, a 186–184 Pistons win in triple overtime.
Answer on page 14.

17. What was the original name of the NBA?
Answer on page 14.

18. Who was the first Australian to play in the NBA?
Answer on page 14.

19. Who was the first African American to play in an NBA game?
Answer on page 14.

20. Kareem Abdul-Jabbar wore No. 33 his 20-season NBA career in honor of his favorite football player. Who was he?
Answer on page 14.

21. Who was the NBA's first unrestricted free agent?
Answer on page 14.

22. In which season did the NBA institute its salary cap?
A. 1946–47
B. 1964–65
C. 1978–79
D. 1983–84
Answer on page 14.

23. Of the first ten players to be named Rookie of the Year (starting in 1958), there is only one who is not in the Hall of Fame. Can you name him?
Answer on page 14–15.

24. What was the original name of the Detroit Pistons?
Answer on page 15.

25. Who was the first New York Knicks player to score 50 or more points in a game?
Answer on page 15.

26. Who was the first Chicago Bulls player to score 50 or more points in a game?
Answer on page 15.

27. Who is credited with making the first basket in what the NBA recognizes as its first game?
Answer on page 15.

28. Which team won the first NBA game?
A. Toronto Huskies
B. New York Knickerbockers
C. Minneapolis Lakers
D. Boston Celtics
Answer on page 15.

29. Who scored the first points of the millennium, on New Year's Day of 2000?
Answer on page 15.

30. This guard has dished the most assists among foreign-born players in NBA history. Who is he?
Answer on page 15.

31. This forward has scored the most points among foreign-born players in NBA history. Who is he?
Answer on page 16.

32. This center has grabbed the most rebounds among foreign-born players in NBA history. Who is he?
Answer on page 16.

33. What about blocks?
Answer on page 16.

34. When the NBA was formed in 1946, it consisted of 11 teams. Four of them lasted only one season. Which teams were they?
Answer on page 16.

35. Which NBA player spent six years as a child in a Japanese internment camp near Tokyo during World War II??
Answer on page 16.

36. Only two teams from the original NBA are still in existence today. Name them.
Answer on page 16.

37. Which NBA team did the Harlem Globetrotters defeat in 1948 to eventually help break the league's color barrier?
Answer on page 17.

38. Who holds the distinction of being the first female to suit up for the Harlem Globetrotters?
A. Ann Meyers
B. Lynette Woodard
C. Nancy Lieberman
D. Jennifer Gillom
Answer on page 17.

39. Who was the first international player in the NBA?
Answer on page 17.

40. Men's basketball was added to the Olympics in 1936, and women's in 1976. Which countries won the gold medals in the respective sports?
Answer on page 17.

41. In the first Olympics to include basketball in 1936, on what surface was the game played?
Answer on page 17.

42. Who became the first woman to sign an NBA contract?
Answer on page 17.

HISTORY

ANSWERS

1. Dr. James Naismith invented "Basket Ball" in 1891, and originally wrote thirteen rules to the game. They are (from Naismith's original draft):

    1. The ball may be thrown in any direction with one or both hands.
    2. The ball may be batted in any direction with one or both hands (never with the fist).
    3. A player cannot run with the ball, the player must throw it from the spot on which he catches it, allowance to be made for a man who catches the ball when running at a good speed.
    4. The ball must be held in or between the hands, the arms or body must not be used for holding it.
    5. No shouldering, holding, pushing, tripping or striking in any way the person of an opponent shall be allowed. The first infringement of this rule by any person shall count as a foul, the second shall disqualify him until the next goal is made, or if there was evident intent to injure the person, for the whole of that game, no substitute allowed.
    6. A foul is striking at the ball with the fist, violation of rules 3 and 4, and such as described in rule 5.
    7. If either side makes three consecutive fouls it shall count a goal for the opponents (consecutive means without the opponents in the meantime making a foul).
    8. A goal shall be made when the ball is thrown or batted from the grounds [into the basket] and stays there, providing those defending the goal do not touch or disturb the goal. If the ball

rests on the edge and the opponent moves the basket it shall count as a goal.

9. When the ball goes out of bounds it shall be thrown into the field, and played by the person first touching it. In case of a dispute the umpire shall throw it straight into the field. The thrower in is allowed five seconds, if he holds it longer it shall go to the opponent. If any side persists in delaying the game, the umpire shall call a foul on them.

10. The umpire shall be judge of the men, and shall note the fouls, and notify the referees when these consecutive fouls have been made. He shall have power to disqualify men according to Rule 5.

11. The referee shall be judge of the ball and shall decide when the ball is in play, in bounds, and to which side it belongs, and shall keep the time. He shall decide when a goal has been made, and keep account of the goals with any other duties that are usually performed by a referee.

12. The time shall be two fifteen minutes halves, with five minutes rest between.

13. The side making the most goals in that time shall be declared the winners. In case of a draw the game may, by agreement of the captains, be continued until another goal is made.

2. Danny Biasone, the founder and owner of the NBA's Syracuse Nationals. He came up with the idea of the 24-second shot clock in 1954 and quickly convinced NBA brass that the clock was crucial to speed the game up. The Hall of Famer owned the Nationals from 1946 to 1963, winning the NBA championship in 1955.

3. The 1954–55 season was the first in which the NBA would have a shot clock.

4. 18 inches.

5. A soccer ball. It was not changed until 1929. G. L. Pierce acquired the US patent for the design of the basketball we know today on June 25, 1929.

6. Maple Leaf Gardens provided the stage for the New York Knicker-bockers to take on the Toronto Huskies on November. 1, 1946.

7. That would be 5-foot-10 Kenny Sailors, who played collegiately at the University of Wyoming, where he led the Cowboys to victories in both the NCAA and the NIT tournaments, and professionally for seven teams, first for the Cleveland Rebels in the 1946–47 season.

8. The Dallas Mavericks were not an original member of the ABA. (A)

9. Artis Gilmore played for the Kentucky Colonels from 1971–72 to 1975–76, before joining the NBA's Chicago Bulls. During his time in the ABA, Gilmore scored a total of 9,362 points, 3,207 more than the second leading scorer Dave Robisch (6,155). (B)

10. Did we trick you? The answer is Artis Gilmore, who had 7,169 rebounds with the Colonels, 3,616 more than Dave Robisch (3,553). (B)

11. Noticing a trend? The answer, once again, is Artis Gilmore, who had 1,273 assists, 390 more than Dave Twardzik (883). (B)

12. If your instinct was to pick Artis Gilmore, you would be incorrect! While Gilmore did play in 420 games—which is second-most—he was two behind Dave Robisch, who played in a total of 422 games. (C)

13. The Spirits of St. Louis. The NBA did not put an end to the agree-ment until 2014, after the Spirits' owners had collected a reported $300 million in television revenue over 38 years. (C)

14. Byron Beck of the Denver Nuggets and Louie Dampier of the Ken-tucky Colonels.

15. Denver Nuggets, Indiana Pacers, New York Nets, and San Antonio Spurs.

16. False. The longest game of the shot-clock era actually happened in November 1989, when the Seattle SuperSonics defeated the Milwaukee Bucks, 155–154, in five overtimes.

17. Well . . . the NBA was the original name. However, the league we know today was born in 1949, when the Basketball Association of America (BAA) merged with the National Basketball League (NBL).

18. Taken in the first round (7th overall) of the 1991 draft, Luc Longley became the first Australian-born player in the NBA. He would go on to win three championships with the Jordan-led Bulls.

19. On October 31, 1950, Earl Lloyd became the first African American to play in an NBA game, doing so with the Washington Capitols.

20. Kareem Abdul-Jabbar's favorite football player was Mel Triplett, a running back for the New York Giants.

21. After two seasons with the San Diego Clippers and five with the Seattle SuperSonics, Tom Chambers signed with the Phoenix Suns in 1988 as the league's first unrestricted free agent.

22. The salary cap has been in place since the first season of the BAA (1946–47), when it stood at $55,000 and most players were paid about $4,000 or $5,000 a year. (A)

23. The ROY for the 1962–63 season was Terry Dischinger, who averaged 25.5 PPG, 8.0 RPG, and 3.1 APG with the Chicago Zephyrs. His first three years were stellar, but would miss two seasons to military service. *However*, while he was not elected to the HOF based on his individual talents, he *was* inducted—along with his teammates—as a member of the 1960 Olympic basketball team, who made their way into the Hall in 2010.

The answer is actually Luke Jackson, who was the 1964–65 ROY with the Philadelphia 76ers. It was also the only time he would be named an All-Star during his eight years in the league, as a major injury in 1969 derailed his career, limiting him to just 66 games in his last three seasons.

24. Fort Wayne Zollner Pistons. Those Pistons, named after owner Fred Zollner, existed from 1941 to 1957 before moving from Indiana to Detroit.

25. Richie Guerin scored 57 points on December 11, 1959, against the Syracuse Nationals.

26. Chet Walker accomplished this feat on February 6, 1972, scoring 56 points in a losing effort against the Cincinnati Royals.

27. Ossie Schectman of the New York Knickerbockers scored the first basket in the league's inaugural game against the Toronto Huskies.

28. The Knicks defeated the Huskies, 68–66, on November 1, 1946. Any fan taller than 6-foot-8 Toronto center George Nostrand was granted free admission. (B)

29. Orlando Magic center John Amaechi, who hit the first basket in the day's first game against the Miami Heat. After the game, Amaechi's jersey and shoes were taken to the Naismith Memorial Basketball Hall of Fame in Springfield, Massachusetts.

30. Only one of five players with more than 10k assists, the Canadian-born Steve Nash, has the most of any foreign-born player in NBA history with 10,335. An 18-year NBA veteran—mostly with the Phoenix Suns and Dallas Mavericks—Nash was one of the best passers the game has ever seen. Rounding out the top five are Tony Parker (7,036, Belgium), José Calderon (5,148, Spain), Manu Ginóbili (4,001, Argentina), and Ricky Rubio (3,817, Spain).

31. Nicknamed the "Dunking Deutschman" and a future Hall of Famer, Dirk Nowitzki scored more than 31k points during his 21-year career—all with the Dallas Mavericks (31,560). Rounding out the top five are Dominique Wilkins (26,668, France), Tim Duncan (26,496, US Virgin Islands), Pau Gasol (20,894, Spain), and Kiki Vandeweghe (15,980, Germany).

32. Did you see your answer in a dream? Well that hint probably gives you the answer, as Nigerian-born Hakeem "The Dream" Olajuwon leads this category with 13,748 rebounds during his 18-year career—all but one with the Houston Rockets. Rounding out the top five are Dikembe Mutombo (12,359, Democratic Republic of the Congo), Patrick Ewing (11,607, Jamaica), Vlade Divac (9,326, Serbia), and Swen Nater (8,340, Netherlands).

33. Did you have another dream? Well, you should have. That's right, Hakeem Olajuwon has the most blocks by any foreign-born player with 3,830. Second on the list is, again, Dikembe Mutombo, who had 3,289 during his 18-year career. In fact, they are number one and two for *all* NBA players, both foreign and domestic. Rounding out the top five are Patrick Ewing (2,894, Jamaica), Shawn Bradley (2,119, Germany), and Manute Bol (2,086, South Sudan). Very interesting that three of the top five were born in Africa.

34. The Cleveland Rebels, the Detroit Falcons, the Pittsburgh Ironmen, and the Toronto Huskies.

35. Tom Meschery, whose parents were Russian emigrants who fled from the October Revolution in 1917. Meschery grew into a 6-foot-6 forward, and was a first-round pick by the Philadelphia Warriors in 1961. He also wrote poetry in his spare time and dedicated one to Warriors teammate Wilt Chamberlain. Meschery coached the ABA's Carolina Cougars following his playing days and had his No. 14 retired by the Warriors.

36. The Boston Celtics and the New York Knicks.

37. The Minneapolis Lakers.

38. Lynette Woodard, in 1985. Prior to joining the Globetrotters, Woodard was a standout at the University of Kansas, going on to being the leading scorer in Italy's women's league. (B)

39. Hank Biasatti was born in Italy and raised in Canada, and played six games for the Toronto Huskies during the 1946–47 season.

40. The USA and USSR, respectively.

41. Outdoors, on clay and sand.

42. Ann Meyers, the 1978 NCAA Division I Player of the Year out of UCLA, signed a $50,000 contract with the Indiana Pacers on September 5, 1979. She survived the first round of cuts before being released.

COLLEGE

QUESTIONS

There was a time, and not long ago, when college basketball was king. Many of the best players stayed all four seasons (or at least two or three) and the game was centered on speed, size and pizzazz.

Today, the college game is still good—but it has undeniably changed. For the past fifteen years or so, it's become known as the "one-and-done" era, where the top stars make themselves eligible for the NBA draft at about the same time the final buzzer sounds on their freshman season.

That has made college basketball almost like minor-league baseball, with the school's name and uniforms being about the only thing that stays the same from year to year. Things have also become considerably more perimeter-oriented, with 7-footers playing further and further away from the basket.

It doesn't necessarily make it better, or worse . . . just different.

But no matter your feelings on how things have changed, there's no doubting the college game remains alive, very well and rich in tradition.

That truth will hopefully be revealed in the following questions, and their answers.

1. Which two teams played in the first men's college basketball game? *Answer on page 27.*

2. What year did the first NCAA tournament take place? *Answer on page 27.*

3. Which teams played for the first NCAA title?
   Answer on page 27.

4. Which player scored the most points in an NCAA tournament game?
   Answer on page 27.

5. Match the player to their college:
   1. Kenny Smith   A. LSU
   2. Kenneth Faried   B. Georgia
   3. Kyle Korver   C. Tennessee
   4. Andrew Bogut   D. UConn
   5. Ray Allen   E. UNC
   6. Bill Bradley   F. Saint Joseph's
   7. Jameer Nelson   G. Creighton
   8. Dominique Wilkins   H. Morehead State
   9. Shaquille O'Neal   I. Utah
   10. Bernard King   J. Stanford
   Answer on page 27.

6. Who is the only player to be named NCAA College Basketball AP Player of the Year three times?
   Answer on page 27.

7. Which player holds the all-time NCAA Division I records for career scoring and average?
   Answer on page 27.

8. Which player holds the all-time NCAA Division I single-season record for most blocks?
   Answer on page 27.

9. Which player holds the all-time NCAA Division I single-season record for blocks per game?
   Answer on page 27–28.

10. Who are the only two freshman to be awarded the Naismith College Player of the Year Award?
Answer on page 28.

11. In 1920, what rule change was implemented?
Answer on page 28.

12. Which college player scored a record 113 points in a game in 1954?
Answer on page 28.

13. What team set a single-game record by scoring 258 points in a game?
Answer on page 28.

14. In 1913, what major rule change was implemented?
Answer on page 28.

15. What school became the first to lose consecutive NCAA tournament championship games?
Answer on page 28.

16. Since the Women's NCAA tournament began in 1982, which school was the first back-to-back winner?
Answer on page 28.

17. Which school women's team was the first back-to-back-to-back National Champion?
Answer on page 28.

18. Which Duke player threw the memorable inbounds pass to Christian Laettner, leading to his buzzer-beating basket against Kentucky in the East regional championship game in 1992?
Answer on page 29.

19. What was the name of Cameron Indoor Stadium prior to 1972?
Answer on page 29.

20. We all know the powerhouse that Geno Auriemma has built at UConn. But do you know how many championhips he's won?
Answer on page 29.

21. In addition, how many of those seasons did his team go undefeated?
Answer on page 29.

22. What was the first school to go undefeated for the season and win the National Championship?
Answer on page 29.

23. Who was the first player to lead Division I basketball in scoring for three consecutive seasons?
Answer on page 29.

24. Which player led Division I in scoring in 1971 by averaging 40.1 points per game?
Answer on page 29.

25. Who was the first ACC player to league the nation in rebounding?
Answer on page 29.

26. Which player has scored the most points in women's NCAA history?
A. Jackie Stiles
B. Brittney Griner
C. Kelsey Plum
D. Kelsey Mitchell
Answer on page 29.

27. Which team was the *last* to win the NCAA tournament title without losing a game?
Answer on page 30.

28. Who was the first Division I player to lead the nation in assists in back-to-back seasons?
Answer on page 30.

29. Which team was the first to win the NCAA tournament with more than six losses for its season?
Answer on page 30.

30. Who was the first Division I player to pass the 1,000-assist mark?
Answer on page 30.

31. Who was the first Division I player to make 400 or more three-pointers?
Answer on page 30.

32. Who is the only person to have played in an NCAA tournament title game *and* a World Series?
Answer on page 30.

33. This center was named National Player of the Year, while averaging only 14.6 points per game. Can you name him?
Answer on page 30.

34. How many consecutive NCAA tournament games did UCLA win, from 1964 to 1974?
Answer on page 30.

35. What is the lowest-seeded team to win the NCAA tournament?
Answer on page 30.

36. The 2008 tournament became the first time all four No. 1 seeds reached the Final Four. Name the four schools.
Answer on page 30.

37. Who was the only player to reach the NCAA tournament title game while playing for more than one school?
Answer on page 31.

38. Which charter member of the Atlantic Coast Conference won the first ACC tournament in 1954?
Answer on page 31.

39. Who is the only No. 16 seed to defeat a No. 1 seed in the NCAA tournament?
Answer on page 31.

40. Where did Dennis Rodman begin his college career?
A. Southwest Missouri State
B. North Central Texas
C. Detroit-Mercy
D. Southeastern Oklahoma State
Answer on page 31.

41. Who has the most assists in NCAA history?
A. Bobby Hurley
B. Ed Cota
C. Bob Cousy
D. Gary Payton
Answer on page 31.

42. Who is the only female player to have more than 2,000 rebounds for their collegiate career?
Answer on page 31.

43. Only one player in NCAA history has shot better than 55 percent on three-pointers for an entire season. Name him.
Answer on page 31.

44. Who led the NCAA in scoring in 2018–19?
Answer on page 31.

45. True or False. Georgetown reached the NCAA championship game in all four of center Patrick Ewing's seasons.
Answer on page 31.

46. Since 1980, only one school has produced the NCAA single-season scoring leader in back-to-back seasons. Name the school.
Answer on page 32.

47. There are only four women who have more than a thousand assists in their collegiate career. Can you name them?
Answer on page 32.

48. Name the only player from the University of Montana to become an NBA All-Star.
Answer on page 32.

49. Which former NCAA scoring champion led the NBA in scoring in 1977?
Answer on page 32.

50. What did the NCAA tournament do away with after the 1981 season?
Answer on page 32.

51. Who was the first player to be named most outstanding player in back-to-back NCAA tournaments?
Answer on page 32.

52. Which team won both the NIT and NCAA tournaments in the same season?
Answer on page 32.

53. Which Arkansas player made a shot from beyond half-court just before the final buzzer to eliminate defending champion Louisville to send the Razorbacks to the Sweet 16 in the 1981 NCAA tournament?
Answer on page 32.

54. Which school was the first to have an all-black starting five?
Answer on page 32.

55. We all know the long-standing rivalry between Duke and UNC. But do you know which school has the most members in the Hall of Fame? (As an individual player, not as part of a team.) *Answer on page 33.*

COLLEGE

ANSWERS

1. Iowa and the University of Chicago squared off on January 18, 1896, in Iowa City. The host team prevailed, 15–12.

2. The first NCAA tournament took place in 1939.

3. The Oregon Webfoots defeated the Ohio State Buckeyes, 46–33, played on the campus of Northwestern University in Evanston, Illinois.

4. Austin Carr, who scored 61 points for Notre Dame vs. Ohio in 1970.

5. 1-E, 2-H, 3-G, 4-I, 5-D, 6-J, 7-F, 8-B, 9-A, 10-C

6. Ralph Sampson was named AP POY in 1981, 1982, and 1983 with the Virginia Cavaliers.

7. "Pistol" Pete Maravich holds the all-time NCAA Division I records for career scoring (3,667) and average (44.2) during his time at LSU.

8. During his 1985–86 season with Navy, "The Admiral" David Robinson recorded 207 blocks in 35 games played.

9. As previously mentioned, Robinson's 207 blocks in 35 games gave him an average of 5.91 BPG. But it's not the highest. That accolade goes to Shawn James, who during his sophomore season with Northeastern

(2005–06) averaged 6.53 blocks per game. He is also 11 blocks behind Robinson (196) for second-most in a single season.

10. In 2007, Texas freshman Kevin Durant was the first to win this illustrious award. The second was Kentucky's Anthony Davis in 2012.

11. The backboard was moved two feet from the wall under the baskets. Previous to that, players could "climb" the wall to make baskets.

12. Bevo Francis did so with the University of Rio Grande. In January 1954, Francis set a collegiate record by scoring 84 points in a game against Alliance College. Two weeks later, on February 2, against Hillsdale College of Michigan, he had 74 points at the beginning of the fourth quarter.

Guarded by three and sometimes four players, he seemingly could not miss. He turned in midair to make twisting jump shots; he sank hook shots from the top of the key. He made 38 field goals and 37 of 45 free throws to finish with 113 points as Rio Grande won, 134–91.

13. Troy University on January 12, 1992, in a 258–141 thrashing of DeVry University.

14. The bottom of the net was left open, which meant it was no longer necessary to retrieve the basketball from the net every time a shot was made.

15. Ohio State, which lost to Cincinnati in the 1961 and 1962 title games.

16. Winning the 1983 and 1984 national championships, the University of Southern California (USC) became the first school to win back-to-back titles.

17. Led by Hall of Fame coach Pat Summitt, the Univerity of Tennessee Lady Vols won the NCAA title in 1996, '97, and '98, becoming the first school to win the women's championship in three consecutive years.

18. That would be Grant Hill.

19. Duke Indoor Stadium.

20 and 21. Geno Auriemma has led his Huskies to domination in women's college basketball. Below are all his titles, with an * next to those undefeated seasons:

1995 (35–0)*	2010 (39–0)*
2000 (36–1)	2013 (35–4)
2002 (39–0)*	2014 (40–0)*
2003 (37–1)	2015 (38–1)
2004 (31–4)	2016 (38–0)*
2009 (39–0)*	

That's right. UConn has won 11 titles under Auriemma, with six of those coming in undefeated seasons.

22. With a 34–0 record, the Texas Longhorns won the 1986 national championship over USC, becoming the first school to win the championship while going undefeated for the season.

23. Oscar Robertson of the University of Cincinnati, doing so from 1958 to 1960.

24. Johnny Neumann of Mississippi.

25. "The Big Fundamental," Tim Duncan of Wake Forest led the nation during his 1996–97 season with 14.7 RPG.

26. Playing for the University of Washington, Kelsey Plum—who was taken No. 1 overall in the 2017 WNBA Draft by the San Antonio Stars—scored 3,527 points during her collegiate career. To go along with that, she also has a gold medal in the 2013 U19 World Championship, a silver in the 2015 Pan American Games, and a gold in the 2018 World Cup (to go along with her other numerous awards). (C)

27. The 1975–76 Indiana Hoosiers, who went 32–0. Bill Russell and the 1956 San Francisco Dons were the first NCAA Division I men's college basketball team to finish the year undefeated with an NCAA tournament championship.

Over the course of the next 20 seasons, six other teams would go on to end the year unblemished. But not one squad has completed the elusive perfect season since Bobby Knight and the Indiana Hoosiers did so in 1976.

28. Avery Johnson did so with Southern in 1987 (10.7) and 1988 (13.3).

29. Al McGuire's Marquette Warriors in 1977, who lost seven games—six of them on their home floor.

30. Chris Corchiani of North Carolina State (1988–1991).

31. Doug Day, who made 401 for Radford University from 1990 to 1993. Since then, 17 different players have made 400 or more three-pointers for their collegiate career. In fact, Fletcher Magee (509, 2016–19; Wofford) and Travis Bader (504, 2011–14; Oakland) are the only two players with 500 or more three-pointers for their careers.

32. Tim Stoddard made the NCAA tournament with NC State in 1974, and the World Series with the Baltimore Orioles in 1979.

33. While only averaging 14.6 PPG, Patrick Ewing of Georgetown University was the POY in 1985.

34. During that 10-year span, the Bruins won a total of 38 consecutive tournament games.

35. In the 1985 title game, No. 8 seeded Villanova pulled off a stunning upset over No. 1 seeded Georgetown, 66–64.

36. Kansas, North Carolina, UCLA, and Memphis.

37. Bob Bender, who was on Indiana's 1976 undefeated championship team and also on Duke's 1978 team, which fell in the title game to Kentucky.

38. In 1954, NC State—under legendary coach Everett Case—defeated Wake Forest in overtime, 82–80, to claim the first ACC tourney crown.

39. On March 16, 2018, the No. 16 seeded University of Maryland, Baltimore County Retrievers (UMBC) defeated the No. 1 seeded Virginia Cavaliers, 74–54. It was the first time in tournament history that a No. 1 seed was upset in the first round. While they would fall to No. 9 Kansas State in the next round, they put up a fight to the bitter end, making tournament history in the process.

40. Transferring to Southeastern Oklahoma State in 1983, Dennis Rodman began his collegiate career at North Central Texas. (B)

41. Bobby Hurley compiled 1,076 assists with Duke from 1989 to 1993. (A)

42. With 2,034 career rebounds, Oklahoma Sooner Courtney Paris is the NCAA all-time leader in rebounds. The next closest is Wanda Ford, who collected 1,887 rebounds with Drake University in the 1980s.

43. Duquesne guard Micah Mason went 118 of 279 on threes during his senior season for a sizzling 56 percent.

44. Campbell guard Chris Clemons, a 5-foot-9 senior, averaged 30.1 points to lead the nation.

45. False. Patrick Ewing and the Hoyas came close, but were eliminated by Memphis State in the second round of the 1983 NCAA tournament. They did reach the championship in each of Ewing's other three seasons, losing to North Carolina in 1982, defeating Houston in 1984, and losing to Villanova in 1985 in a game many still consider as the greatest title game upset in tournament history.

46. Loyola-Marymount. The late Hank Gathers led the nation in scoring in 1988–89 with an average of 32.7 points per game. The next season, Gathers's teammate and close friend Bo Kimble repeated the feat at 35.3 PPG.

47. As mentioned, there are only four women who have more than one thousand assists in their collegiate career. They are: Suzie McConnell (1,307, Penn State), Andrea Nagy (1,165, Florida International), Courtney Vandersloot (1,118, Gonzaga), and Tine Freil (1,088, Pacific).

48. Micheal Ray Richardson, who was selected as an All-Star three times as a member of the New York Knicks (1979–80, 1980–81, 1981–82), and once more with the New Jersey Nets (1984–85).

49. Pete Maravich, who averaged 31.6 points with the New Orleans Jazz.

50. The last consolation game, featuring the Final Four losers playing a game for third place. Virginia defeated Louisiana State, 78–74.

51. Bob Kurland of Oklahoma State in 1945 and 1946.

52. The once-powerhouse City College of New York (CCNY) did so in 1949–50.

53. U. S. Reed.

54. On March 19, 1966, Texas Western (now known as Texas-El Paso) coach Don Haskins put out the first all-black starting five in collegiate history. The Miners were led by Bobby Joe Hill, Willie Worsley, Harry Flournoy, David Lattin, and Orsten Artis. While they had to overcome issues of race—mostly in southern states—whey would go on to the national championship against the top-ranked Kentucky Wildcats. The Miners would win the game, 72–65, taking the national title. The team was inducted into the Naismith Memorial Basketball Hall of Fame in 2007, and inspired the book and film *Glory Road*.

55. Would you believe that it's not even close? Duke University has a total of one—yes, one—Blue Devil in the Hall of Fame. That would be Grant Hill, who was elected in 2018. The University of North Carolina, on the other hand, has a total of six Tar Heels in the HOF. They are: Billy Cunningham (1986), Bob McAdoo (2000), James Worthy (2003), Michael Jordan (2009), Charlie Scott (2018), and Bobby Jones (2019).

DRAFT

QUESTIONS

The NBA draft is a time for bad teams to dream. It's a time for prospects to think about becoming the league's "Next Big Thing." It's a time for fans to watch their favorite college (or sometimes high school) players take center stage, and perhaps don the cap of their favorite pro team.

The draft has been around as long as the NBA itself, but it was never given much thought until it became a David Stern Production. Stern was NBA commissioner from 1984 to 2014, and he turned the draft into must-see TV. It was under Stern's watch that the league came up with the draft lottery—a system in which the worst teams have their logos placed on Ping Pong balls and thrown into a hopper. Whichever logo comes out at the right time gets the No. 1 overall pick. That process even has its own show, with the lottery broadcast in mid-May, usually ahead of a playoff game.

Then comes the night of the actual draft in June. Stern put himself at center stage, calling out the name of each team, their pick . . . then the player they have selected. (Current commissioner Adam Silver has inherited those honors.) It can be high drama, as teams don't always select the expected prospect.

But no matter how you spin it, the fact about the draft is the right pick can change the fortunes of a team. The wrong one can, too. What follows are some of the more and less notable ones throughout history.

1. Excluding recently drafted players, name the No. 1 overall picks who appeared in less than 150 career games.
   Answer on page 43.

People can always remember when the big-name stars were drafted, but how well do you know about the forgotten picks?

2. In the 2007 NBA Draft, Kevin Durant was taken No. 2 overall by the Seattle Sonics. Who was No. 1?
   Answer on page 43.

3. In the 2003 NBA Draft, LeBron James was taken No. 1 overall by the Cleveland Cavaliers, and Carmelo Anthony was taken No. 3 by the Denver Nuggets. Who was No. 2?
   Answer on page 43.

4. In the 1993 NBA Draft, Chris Webber was taken No. 1 overall out of Michigan. What team drafted him? In addition, who was the No. 2 pick?
   Answer on page 43.

5. In the 1992 NBA Draft, college great Christian Laettner was drafted No. 3 overall by the Minnesota Timberwolves. Which two future Hall of Famers were drafted No. 1 and No. 2?
   Answer on page 44.

6. In the 1984 NBA Draft, the great Michael Jordan was drafted No. 3 overall by the Chicago Bulls out of UNC. Who were the No. 1 and No. 2 picks? Hint, one would become a Hall of Famer.
   Answer on page 44.

7. In addition, who was selected fourth in that famed draft, one pick after Michael Jordan and one ahead of Charles Barkley?
   Answer on page 44.

8. Which of the following was the first-ever draft pick in Cleveland Cavaliers history?
   A. John Johnson
   B. Austin Carr
   C. Bubbles Harris
   D. Dave Sorenson
   Answer on page 44.

9. Which of the following was the first-ever draft pick in Phoenix Suns history?
   A. Neal Walk
   B. Dick Cunningham
   C. Gar Heard
   D. Gary Gregor
   Answer on page 44.

10. Which former No. 4 overall draft pick was selected by the Charlotte Bobcats in the 2004 expansion draft?
    Answer on page 44.

11. What team drafted Dirk Nowitzki with the No. 9 overall pick of the 1998 NBA Draft?
    Answer on page 44.

12. Who was the first lottery draft pick in NBA history?
    Answer on page 44.

13. Who was the first player to be drafted out of high school?
    Answer on page 44.

14. Who was the first No. 1 overall pick to be drafted straight from high school?
    Answer on page 44.

15. From 2001 to 2006, there was only one player drafted No. 1 overall that attended college. Can you name him, and what year he was drafted? Can you name the other four (excluding the answer to the question above), what year they were drafted, and what high school/country they came from?
Answer on page 45.

16. Match the All-Star with the NBA team that drafted them:
1. Kobe Bryant   A. Milwaukee Bucks
2. Ray Allen   B. Memphis Grizzlies
3. Kevin Love   C. Minnesota Timberwolves
4. Dominique Wilkins   D. Charlotte Hornets
5. Julius Erving   E. Utah Jazz
Answer on page 45.

17. Match the 1984 draft pick with his college.
1. Michael Jordan   A. Ohio State
2. Hakeem Olajuwon   B. Michigan
3. Otis Thorpe   C. Providence
4. Tim McCormick   D. Cal State Fullerton
5. Michael Cage   E. San Diego State
6. Vern Fleming   F. Houston
7. Tony Campbell   G. North Carolina
8. Leon Wood   H. Georgia
Answer on page 45.

18. Who was the youngest player ever drafted?
A. Spencer Haywood
B. Andrew Bynum
C. Darko Miličić
D. Kobe Bryant
Answer on page 45.

19. Who was the tallest player ever drafted?
Answer on page 45.

20. Who was the shortest player ever drafted?
Answer on page 45.

21. Which six franchises have never had the No. 1 overall draft pick (through the 2019 draft)?
Answer on page 45.

22. Who is the only second-round pick to go on to win league MVP?
Answer on page 45.

23. How many rounds were there in the 1968 draft?
A. 3
B. 10
C. 21
D. 30
Answer on page 46.

24. In 1998, one team offered a combination of any five players and two first-round draft picks to the Chicago Bulls for Michael Jordan. Do you know which team?
Answer on page 46.

25. Who was the last four-year college player to be selected with the No. 1 overall draft pick (through the 2019 draft)?
Answer on page 46.

26. Who was the first player born outside of the United States to be selected with the No. 1 overall pick?
Answer on page 46.

27. Which franchise has had the most No. 1 overall picks through the 2019 draft?
Answer on page 46.

28. Who was the last player, before Anthony Davis in 2012, to be drafted No. 1 overall after playing on an NCAA championship team?
    Answer on page 46.

29. Which player was selected two picks after first overall pick Tim Duncan in 1997, and went on to win a Finals MVP?
    Answer on page 46.

30. What NBA general manager/president was drafted by the Boston Celtics in the second round of the 1981 draft, but at first opted to play professional baseball instead?
    Answer on page 46.

31. Which player was drafted No. 6 overall as a college junior in 1978, but went on to play his senior season anyway?
    Answer on page 46–47.

32. Who was selected with the No. 2 overall pick behind Magic Johnson in 1979?
    Answer on page 47.

33. Which city has produced the most overall No. 1 draft picks?
    Answer on page 47.

34. Hall of Famer Bill Russell was drafted by which team?
    Answer on page 47.

35. Who was selected with the No. 1 overall pick, one spot ahead of Bill Russell, in the 1956 draft?
    Answer on page 47.

36. Who were the two Hall of Famers drafted by the Boston Celtics in 1956?
    Answer on page 47.

37. Who was the first player in NBA draft history to be taken with the No. 1 overall pick?
Answer on page 47.

38. In the same draft they selected Michael Jordan (1984), the Chicago Bulls also selected a nine-time Olympic gold-medal winner. Who was he?
Answer on page 47.

39. Which future Hall of Famer was the No. 1 overall pick in the 2004 WNBA Draft?
Answer on page 47.

40. Who was the first woman ever selected in an NBA draft?
Answer on page 47–48.

DRAFT

ANSWERS

1. 1948: Andy Tonkovich, 17; 1952: Mark Workman, 79; 2007: Greg Oden, 105; 1949: Howie Shannon, 122; 1963: Art Heyman, 147.

2. In the 2007 draft, Greg Oden was taken No. 1 overall by the Portland Trail Blazers out of Ohio State. Oden only started in 66 games over his career, missing half his time (three of six years) due to injury. He would be out of the NBA by age 26.

3. In the 2003 draft, Darko Miličić was taken No. 2 overall by the Detroit Pistons out of Serbia. Though Miličić would play in 10 NBA seasons, he was known more for being a bust and not living up to the huge potential expected of him (especially being the sandwich pick between LeBron and 'Melo). The Pistons would ship him to Orlando in only his third season, and he'd go on to play for four other teams, never coming close to his full potential.

4. In the 1993 draft, Chris Webber was taken No. 1 overall by the Orlando Magic out of Michigan, who traded him that night to the Golden State Warriors in exchange for Anfernee "Penny" Hardaway and three first-round picks. Webber would be traded again the following year to the Washington Bullets in exchange for Tom Gugliotta and, again, three first-round picks. The second overall pick in the 1993 draft was Shawn Bradley by the Phoenix Suns out of BYU.

5. In the 1992 draft, Shaquille O'Neal was drafted No. 1 by the Orlando Magic out of LSU, and Alonzo Mourning was taken No. 2 by the Charlotte Hornets out of Georgetown.

6. In the 1984 draft, Hakeem Olajuwon was taken No. 1 overall by the Houston Rockets out of Houston. He would go on to have an 18-year career, being a 12-time All Star, MVP, and two-time NBA champion. The No. 2 pick was Sam Bowie, who taken by the Portland Trail Blazers out of Kentucky. Bowie would play for 10 seasons, most of them injury-plagued, as he never lived up to expectation and will always be remembered as the player picked before Jordan.

7. Sam Perkins, Jordan's teammate at North Carolina, who was drafted by the Dallas Mavericks. Perkins had a productive 17-year career, but never made an All-Star team.

8. The Cavs selected John Johnson with the No. 7 overall pick in their expansion year of 1970. (A)

9. The Suns drafted Gary Gregor with the No. 7 overall pick in 1968. (D)

10. Marcus Fizer, originally taken fourth by the Chicago Bulls in 2000.

11. The Milwaukee Bucks, who traded him—along with Pat Garrity—to the Dallas Mavericks for Robert "Tractor" Traylor.

12. In the 1985 draft, the first year that the NBA began the lottery system, the New York Knicks drafted Patrick Ewing from Georgetown with the No. 1 overall pick.

13. In the 1974 ABA Draft, the Utah Stars selected Moses Malone with their third-round pick, making him "the first high schooler in modern basketball to go directly to the pros," per the *New York Times*.

14. In the 2001 NBA Draft, Kwame Brown was drafted No. 1 overall by the Washington Wizards out of Glynn Academy in Brunswick, Georgia.

15. In the 2005 draft, the Milwaukee Bucks drafted Andrew Bogut from the University of Utah.

In the 2002 draft, the Houston Rockets selected Yao Ming from Shanghai, China; in the 2003 draft, the Cleveland Cavaliers drafted LeBron James from Saint Vincent-Saint Mary in Akron, Ohio; in the 2004 draft the Orlando Magic selected Dwight Howard from Southwest Atlanta Christian Academy in Atlanta, Georgia; and in the 2006 draft the Toronto Raptors drafted Andrea Bargnani from Rome, Italy.

A fun fact is that Bogut, the only player in that six-year span drafted out of college, is originally from Melbourne, Australia.

16. 1-D, 2-C, 3-B, 4-E, 5-A

17. 1-G, 2-F, 3-C, 4-B, 5-E, 6-H, 7-A, 8-D

18. Andrew Bynum was drafted 10th overall by the Los Angeles Lakers in 2005 at the age of 17 years and 249 days. (B)

19. Selected by the Golden State Warriors in the eighth round (171st overall) of the 1981 draft, Japanese center Yasutaka Okayama is the tallest player ever drafted at 7-foot-8. Though being drafted, he did not sign with the Warriors and never played in the NBA.

20. Tyrone "Muggsy" Bogues, a 5-foot-3 point guard, was selected by the Washington Bullets with the No. 12 overall pick in 1987. Bogues went on to have a productive career as a starter, mostly with the Charlotte Hornets, and even earned a role in the 1996 film *Space Jam*.

21. Oklahoma City Thunder, Indiana Pacers, Memphis Grizzlies, Miami Heat, and Denver Nuggets.

22. Willis Reed. Of course, when Reed was drafted there were only seven first-round picks. He went eighth to the Knicks out of Grambling State in 1964, and won the NBA MVP Award in 1970.

23. The 1968 draft consisted of a whopping 21 rounds, with most (but strangely, not all) rounds consisting of 14 picks. A total of 214 players were drafted, with 50 playing in the NBA, though none that were taken beyond the eighth round. (C)

24. That would be the Los Angeles Clippers who were denied. It's probably a good thing, as Jordan retired (for the second time) a year later.

25. Kenyon Martin, who was selected by the New Jersey Nets out of Cincinnati in 2000.

26. Mychal Thompson, who went first overall to the Los Angeles Lakers in 1978. Thompson, the father of Golden State Warriors guard Klay Thompson, was born in the Bahamas.

27. The Cleveland Cavaliers, with six. They used those picks on Austin Carr (1971), Brad Daugherty (1986), LeBron James (2003), Kyrie Irving (2011), Anthony Bennett (2013), and Andrew Wiggins (2014).

28. That would be Grandmama himself, Larry Johnson, who was selected first overall by the Charlotte Hornets in 1991. That was more than a year after Johnson led UNLV to the NCAA championship in 1990. The Runnin' Rebels lost to Duke in the Final Four in 1991.

29. Chauncey Billups, chosen third by the Boston Celtics. He was named Finals MVP as a member of the Detroit Pistons in 2004. The Pistons stunned the Los Angeles Lakers in that year's Finals, a series that earned Billups the nickname "Mr. Big Shot."

30. Danny Ainge, who is currently in charge of the Boston Celtics. He had a short stint with baseball's Toronto Blue Jays before winning championships as a player with the Celtics in 1984 and '86.

31. Larry Bird, who led Indiana State to the 1979 NCAA championship, where his team lost to Magic Johnson and Michigan State, after being drafted by the Boston Celtics. Bird was drafted as a "junior eligible." That odd rule has since been eliminated.

32. David Greenwood, who was taken by the Chicago Bulls.

33. Melbourne, Australia, with three: Andrew Bogut (2005, Milwaukee Bucks), Kyrie Irving (2011, Cleveland Cavaliers), and Ben Simmons (2016, Philadelphia 76ers).

34. The St. Louis Hawks, who used the No. 2 overall pick to select Bill Russell out of San Francisco in 1956. They traded him to the Boston Celtics for Ed Macauley and Cliff Hagan that same day.

35. Duquesne guard Sihugo Green, by the Rochester Royals. Green went on to put together a fairly nondescript career, averaging 9.2 points, 4.3 rebounds, and 3.3 assists with four teams in nine NBA seasons.

36. Tommy Heinsohn and K. C. Jones. Bill Russell, Heinsohn, and Jones all went on to coach the Celtics. (As an aside, Russell and Jones also coached the Seattle SuperSonics.)

37. Chuck Share, a 6-foot-11, 235-pound center who was selected by the Boston Celtics out of Bowling Green State University on April 25, 1950. Share never played a game for Boston, as he was traded to the Fort Wayne Pistons for Bill Sharman the following day.

38. Track star Carl Lewis, whom Chicago took in the 10th round of the draft.

39. After three NCAA championships with UConn, Diana Taurasi was selected first overall by the Phoenix Mercury in the 2004 WNBA Draft.

40. Delta State guard Lusia Harris was drafted by the New Orleans Jazz in the seventh round (137th overall) in 1977. Harris did not have an interest in the NBA, and so declined to try out for the Jazz. She had represented the United States in the 1976 Olympics, taking silver in the first-ever women's Olympic basketball tournament. Considered one of the pioneers of women's basketball, Harris was inducted into the Naismith Memorial Basketball Hall of Fame—the first of two women ever inducted (1992), and one of twenty-six inaugural inductees into the Women's Basketball Hall of Fame (1998).

SECOND QUARTER

ROOKIES

QUESTIONS

There are several types of rookies in the NBA:

1. The type who are selected near the top of the draft and immediately become the face of the franchise. Think Magic Johnson, Larry Bird, Michael Jordan, LeBron James, Kareem Abdul-Jabbar, and beyond.
2. Those drafted later, who no one really knew heading into the draft, but make an immediate impact anyway. More recent examples include Giannis Antetokounmpo, Dirk Nowitzki, Paul George, and Kawhi Leonard.
3. The second-round steals—Dennis Rodman, Draymond Green, and Manu Ginóbili, to name a few.
4. And of course, the type of pick nobody wants. That would be none other than the rookie selected near the top of the draft who fails to live up to the high hopes. Kwame Brown, Anthony Bennett, Michael Olowokandi, Darko Miličić, and Greg Oden are names you may know for all the wrong reasons.

In a lot of cases, rookies have to perform chores for the veterans. They can be charged with running errands, delivering food to the locker room, or as was the case with James's team once in Cleveland, taking care of baby dolls for the entire season. At least, that's the rumor.

But no matter the role off the court, teams rely on rookies to develop, contribute and earn their newfound paychecks from the very minute they step on the court in training camp.

Let's see how much you know about the first-year players who teams hoped could make a difference

1. Which of the following did *not* win the NBA Rookie of the Year Award?
   A Rick Barry
   B David Robinson
   C Anthony Davis
   D Kevin Durant
   Answer on page 59.

2. Which NBA rookie was sidelined during the 1990–91 season with a wrist injury reportedly sustained by playing his Nintendo Game Boy too much?
   Answer on page 59.

3. Who is the only rookie to average:
   10 points per game
   5 assists per game
   5 rebounds per game
   2 steals per game
   A. Deron Williams
   B. Chris Paul
   C. Jason Kidd
   D. Oscar Robertson
   Answer on page 59.

4. Which player had the most triple-doubles in their rookie season?
   A. Magic Johnson
   B. Jason Kidd
   C. Ben Simmons
   D. Oscar Robertson
   Answer on page 59.

5. How many points did Michael Jordan score in his NBA debut?
   Answer on page 59.

6. Who was the first NBA rookie to average 30 or more points per game in their first full season?
Answer on page 59.

7. Who is the all-time rookie single-season scoring leader?
A. George Mikan
B. Wilt Chamberlain
C. Lew Alcindor (Kareem Abdul-Jabbar)
D. Oscar Robertson
Answer on page 60.

8. Who is second among all-time rookie single-season scoring leaders?
A. Walt Bellamy
B. Michael Jordan
C. Geoff Petrie
D. Sidney Wicks
Answer on page 60.

9. Who has the highest field goal percentage during their rookie season?
Answer on page 60.

10. Which player holds the record for most three-pointers made during their rookie season?
Answer on page 60.

11. Who holds the record for highest playoff points per game by a rookie?
Answer on page 60.

12. Who was the first rookie to record a triple-double in the playoffs?
A. Lew Alcindor (Kareem Abdul-Jabbar)
B. Jerry Lucas
C. Magic Johnson
D. Tom Gola
Answer on page 60.

13. Who holds the record for assists per game during their rookie season?
A. John Stockton
B. Magic Johnson
C. Scott Skiles
D. Mark Jackson
Answer on page 60.

14. Who was the youngest rookie to start the first game of the season?
Answer on page 60.

15. Which player averaged the most steals per game by a rookie?
A. Alvin Robertson
B. Dudley Bradley
C. Jeff Cook
D. Geoff Houston
Answer on page 60.

16. Who compiled the most steals in a single game by a rookie?
A. Charles Barkley
B. Ron Harper
C. Scottie Pippen
D. Shawn Marion
Answer on page 60.

17. Who holds the record for most blocked shots in a game by a rookie?
Answer on page 61.

18. Which two players are tied for the rookie record of assists in a game with 25 apiece?
Answer on page 61.

19. Who is the youngest rookie to record a triple-double?
Answer on page 61.

20. Which rookie holds the record for consecutive 40-plus point games with five?
A. Michael Jordan
B. Allen Iverson
C. Rick Barry
D. Wilt Chamberlain
Answer on page 61.

21. Which player holds the record for most points scored in his rookie debut?
A. Julius Erving
B. Wilt Chamberlain
C. Bernard King
D. Shaquille O'Neal
Answer on page 61.

22. Which player holds the rookie-record for most consecutive games hitting a three-pointer?
A. Dell Curry
B. Wesley Matthews
C. Rudy Fernández
D. Michael Finley
Answer on page 61.

23. Who holds the record for most rebounds in one game as a rookie?
Answer on page 61.

24. Name the only two rookies in league history to have compiled seven straight games of 23 or more points.
Answer on page 61.

25. The Toronto Raptors were led by a rookie in scoring during the 1995–96 season. Can you name him?
Answer on page 62.

26. Who holds the record for highest free throw percentage in their rookie season?
A. Ernie DiGregorio
B. Mark Price
C. Rick Barry
D. Stephen Curry
Answer on page 62.

27. Which player bested Oscar Robertson's record for most assists as a rookie?
A. John Stockton
B. Mark Jackson
C. Chris Paul
D. Tim Hardaway
Answer on page 62.

28. Which NBA rookie recorded a triple-double in the first game of their career?
A. Magic Johnson
B. Grant Hill
C. Oscar Robertson
D. Wilt Chamberlain
Answer on page 62.

29. Which player holds the NBA record for most blocked shots in a season as a rookie?
A. Mark Eaton
B. Rudy Gobert
C. Manute Bol
D. Dikembe Mutombo
Answer on page 62.

30. Which player holds the NBA rookie record for most points in a game, scoring 58 twice?
A. Rick Barry
B. Kobe Bryant
C. Michael Jordan
D. Wilt Chamberlain
Answer on page 62.

ROOKIES

ANSWERS

1. Of the group mentioned, Anthony Davis is the only play not to win Rookie of the Year. (C)

2. Lionel Simmons of the Sacramento Kings.

3. In the 2005–06 season with the New Orleans/Oklahoma City Hornets, Chris Paul averaged 16.1 PPG, 7.8 APG, 5.1 RPG, and 2.2 SPG. (B)

4. While Jason Kidd (four), Magic Johnson (seven), and Ben Simmons (eight) all had stellar rookie seasons (with Kidd and Simmons winning ROY honors), the Big O had an outrageous 26 games in which he had 10 or more points, rebounds, and assists during his rookie season. Robertson played in 71 games during the 1960–61 season, which means he got a triple-double in more than a third of all games played! To put that in perspective, it took Russell Westbrook—the last player to average a triple-double for an entire season—eight seasons to surpass Robertson's rookie year numbers. (D)

5. Jordan scored 16 points on 5 of 16 shooting in the Chicago Bulls' 109–93 victory over the Washington Bullets on October 26, 1984.

6. That would be Walt Bellamy, who averaged 31.6 points per game in 1961–62 with the Chicago Packers.

7. That would be Wilt Chamberlain, who averaged 37.6 points per game in 1959–60 with the Philadelphia Warriors. (B)

8. In the 1959–60 season, Wilt Chamberlain scored 2,707 points as a rookie. Second on the all-time list is Walt Bellamy, who scored 2,495. (A)

9. Steve Johnson of the 1981–82 Kansas City Kings, who shot .613 from the floor in his first NBA season.

10. While Portland's Damian Lillard set the record in 2012–13 with 185 three-pointers (breaking Stephen Curry's record of 166, set 2010), Donovan Mitchell of the Utah Jazz buried 187 during his 2017–18 rookie season. Impressively, the top six in this category are all from the past twenty years!

11. Lew Alcindor (Kareem Abdul-Jabbar), who averaged 35.2 points in 10 playoff games with the 1969–70 Milwaukee Bucks.

12. While Magic Johnson recorded five—count them, five—triple-doubles as a rookie in the playoffs, he was far from the first. That distinction goes to Tom Gola, who on March 27, 1956, recorded 16 points, 13 rebounds, and 10 assists as his Philadelphia Warriors defeated the Syracuse Nationals in Game Three of the 1956 Eastern Division finals. (D)

13. Mark Jackson averaged 10.6 assists per game as a rookie with the New York Knicks in 1987–88. (D)

14. LeBron James, who was 18 years and 303 days old when his Cleveland Cavaliers visited the Sacramento Kings on October 29, 2003. He played 42 minutes in that game, putting up 25 points with nine assists, six rebounds, and four steals.

15. Dudley Bradley averaged 2.57 steals per game for the Indiana Pacers in 1979–80. (B)

16. As a rookie with the Cleveland Cavaliers, Ron Harper recorded 10 steals in a game vs. the Philadelphia 76ers on March 10, 1987. (B)

Rookies: Answers

17. Manute Bol of the Washington Bullets, who swatted a whopping 15 shots in a game against the Atlanta Hawks on January 25, 1986.

18. On January 1, 1974, Ernie DiGregorio of the Buffalo Braves dished 25 assists against the Portland Trail Blazers; on February 23, 1987, Nate McMillan of the Seattle SuperSonics dished 25 assists against the Los Angeles Clippers.

19. Philadelphia 76ers guard and 2017 No. 1 overall pick Markelle Fultz compiled 13 points, 10 rebounds, and 10 assists in a game against the Milwaukee Bucks at the age of 19 years and 317 days. Fultz accomplished the feat on April 11, 2018—the last game of the regular season, but only his 14th appearance.

20. The answer is . . . The Answer! Allen Iverson accomplished the feat from April 7 to 14 of 1997. During that stretch, he erupted for 44, 40, 44, 50, and 40 points, respectively. Interestingly, his Philadelphia 76ers lost all five of those games (by an average of 15.4 points). (B)

21. Wilt Chamberlain went for 43 points in his first game with the Philadelphia Warriors on October 24, 1959, in a road win against the New York Knicks. He also pulled down an astounding 28 rebounds. (B)

22. Rudy Fernández made at least one three-pointer in 33 consecutive games as a member of the Portland Trail Blazers, from December 7, 2008, through February 22, 2009. (C)

23. While we previously told you that Wilt grabbed 28 rebounds in his rookie debut, he hauled in 45 boards against the Syracuse Nationals on February 6, 1960, the most by a rookie in league history.

24. Tim Duncan of the San Antonio Spurs (in games 76 to 82 of the 1997–98 season) and Collin Sexton of the Cleveland Cavaliers (in games 66 to 72 of the 2018–19 season).

25. That rookie was Damon Stoudamire, who averaged a team-high 19.0 points in 70 games.

26. Hitting 174 of 193 free throws for the 1973–74 Buffalo Braves, Ernie DiGregorio shot 90.2 percent from the charity stripe, the highest percentage for a rookie in league history. (A)

27. Not only did Mark Jackson surpass Oscar Robertson's 690 assists as a rookie, but he demolished it. In the 1987–88 season, as a member of the New York Knicks, Jackson collected 868 assists in his rookie campaign. (B)

28. With 21 points, 12 rebounds, and 10 assists for the Cincinnati Royals, who defeated the Los Angeles Lakers on October 19, 1960, Oscar Robertson recorded a triple-double in his first career game. It would be the first of twenty-six that he would record that season. (C)

29. In the 1985–86 season, Washington Bullets center Manute Bol blocked 397 shots. The next closest is David Robinson, who swatted 319 during the 1989–90 season. (C)

30. On January 25, 1960, Wilt Chamberlain scored 58 points against the Detroit Pistons, leading his Philadelphia Warriors to a 127–117 victory. Seventeen games later, on February 21, Chamberlain would *again* put up 58 points, this time in a win over the New York Knicks, 129–122. In total, Chamberlain had five games in his rookie season where he scored 50 or more points. (D)

PLAYERS

QUESTIONS

They say pro basketball has always been a players' league and anyone who sees how much of a difference one player can make likely concedes.

After all, how many titles would the Chicago Bulls have won without Michael Jordan— regardless of who was coach? And anyone who follows the sport has seen the modern-day Cleveland Cavaliers without LeBron James. And Jordan and James are just recent examples.

Truth is, in a sport where each team has just five players on the floor at the same time, well, one or two guys can make all the difference.

But in the NBA, there is no prototype. Some players could beat you with a skyhook. Some with speed. Some with otherworldly perimeter shooting.

The best of the best could do it all—mastering every area of the game's fundamentals and being blessed with the right combination of size and strength.

These are the men who make the game worth watching, the men who sell the tickets and decide which merchandise is moved. They are the players and they are who makes the basketball world go 'round.

What follows are some questions and answers on those who made pro basketball what it is today.

1. Match the player with the team he finished his NBA career with:
   1. Patrick Ewing   A. Los Angeles Clippers
   2. Robert Parish   B. New Jersey Nets
   3. Grant Hill   C. Miami Heat
   4. Phil Jackson   D. Orlando Magic
   5. Penny Hardaway   E. Chicago Bulls
   Answer on page 73.

2. Before Stephen Curry broke the record for most three-point field goals (and then broke his own record, and then broke his own record), who held the record?
Answer on page 73.

3. Four players have played for 12 different franchises during their careers. Can you name them? Can you name the teams?
Answer on page 73–74.

4. Which point guard had the most total assists from 2000 to 2010?
A. Steve Nash
B. Andre Miller
C. Jason Kidd
D. Baron Davis
Answer on page 74.

5. Which played has the most 20-20 games (points and rebounds) of all time?
A. Kareem Abdul-Jabbar
B. Hakeem Olajuwon
C. Wilt Chamberlain
D. Bill Russell
Answer on page 74.

6. Which player has the most 20-20 games (points and assists) of all time?
A. Isiah Thomas
B. Oscar Robertson
C. John Stockton
D. Magic Johnson
Answer on page 74.

7. Who has the most triples-doubles in their career?
A. Oscar Robertson
B. Magic Johnson

C. Jason Kidd
D. Russell Westbrook
Answer on page 74.

8. Who is the only player to average 10 or more assists and less than two turnovers a game for an entire season?
   A. John Stockton
   B. Chris Paul
   C. Muggsy Bogues
   D. Doc Rivers
   Answer on page 75.

9. Who is the only player to have a 20-20-20 game (points-rebounds-assists) in their career?
   A. Shaquille O'Neal
   B. Patrick Ewing
   C. Wilt Chamberlain
   D. Bill Russell
   Answer on page 75.

10. Who has the record for blocks in a game?
    A. Manute Bol
    B. Dikembe Mutombo
    C. Shaquille O'Neal
    D. Elmore Smith
    Answer on page 75.

11. Who holds the season record for highest free throw percentage (minimum 65 games)?
    A. Ray Allen
    B. José Calderon
    C. Jeff Hornacek
    D. Mahmoud Abdul-Rauf
    Answer on page 75.

12. Who are the only two players to ever average for a single season:
    25+ PPG
    8+ APG
    7+ RPG

    A. Michael Jordan   F. Kobe Bryant
    B. Larry Bird   G. Russell Westbrook
    C. Magic Johnson   H. Bill Walton
    D. Lebron James   I. Kevin Garnett
    E. James Harden   J. Charles Barkley
    Answer on page 75.

13. Which guard has the most games with 10 or more turnovers?
    A. Isiah Thomas
    B. Dwyane Wade
    C. Russell Westbrook
    D. Deron Williams
    Answer on page 75.

14. Former Orlando Magic guard Scott Skiles set the single-game record for assists with 30 against the Denver Nuggets in December 1990. Which player is second with 29 in a game?
    A. Bob Cousy
    B. John Stockton
    C. Kevin Porter
    D. Guy Rodgers
    Answer on page 75.

15. Who is the player with the most career points who never played in college?
    Answer on page 75.

16. Kobe Bryant was one of the most prolific scorers in NBA history. Playing for 20 seasons, Bryant started 1,198 games. But was he ever held scoreless? How many games, if any, was Kobe held scoreless when he was listed as a starter?
A. None
B. 15 games
C. 3 games
D. 8 games
Answer on page 76.

17. In the 18 regular-season and 19 playoff games, who won more head-to-head matchups between Larry Bird and Magic Johnson?
Answer on page 76.

18. Only one player in NBA history has worn No. 81. Who was it?
A. Dennis Rodman
B. Jordan McRae
C. Nemanja Bjelica
D. José Calderon
Answer on page 76.

19. Wilt Chamberlain, Bill Russell, and Kareem Abdul-Jabbar, respectively, are the top three placers in all-time career rebounds. Who is fourth?
A. Tim Duncan
B. Elvin Hayes
C. Moses Malone
D. Kevin Garnett
Answer on page 76.

20. Which player is the NBA's all-time steals leader?
A. John Stockton
B. Michael Jordan
C. Maurice Cheeks
D. Gary Payton
Answer on page 76.

21. Which player compiled the most steals in a single season?
A. Don Buse
B. Alvin Robertson
C. Chris Paul
D. LeBron James
Answer on page 76.

22. True or False. Then-Cleveland Cavaliers star LeBron James led the league in field goal attempts during the 2017–18 season.
Answer on page 76.

23. Which player is the NBA's all-time leader in three-point field goal percentage?
A. Hubert Davis
B. Stephen Curry
C. Steve Kerr
D. Kyle Korver
Answer on page 76.

24. Which retired player has the highest field goal percentage?
A. Artis Gilmore
B. Shaquille O'Neal
C. Kareem Abdul-Jabbar
D. Darryl Dawkins
Answer on page 77.

25. Only one player has worn the No. 99. Can you name him?
Answer on page 77.

26. Who led the NBA in three-pointers made for the 2017–18 season?
Answer on page 77.

27. Wilt Chamberlain set the still-standing NBA single-game rebounding record of 55 on November 24, 1960. What team did he accomplish this feat against?
Answer on page 77.

28. Who was the first NBA player to shoot better than 90 percent from the free throw line for a season?
Answer on page 77.

29. Which player was the first to average more than 30 points in a season?
Answer on page 77.

30. The NBA did not begin to track blocked shots as an official statistic until the 1973–74 season. Who led the league in rejections that season?
Answer on page 77.

31. Who was the first player to average 10 or more assists per game for a season?
Answer on page 77.

32. Can you name the player that broke *two* backboards in *one* ABA game?
Answer on page 77.

33. Which player has been ejected the most times in NBA history?
Answer on page 77.

34. Who has been slapped with the most technical fouls in a single season?
Answer on page 77.

35. Who made the first three-pointer in NBA history?
Answer on page 78.

36. Who is the only player to lead the NBA in scoring and assists in the same season?
Answer on page 78.

37. This player led the NBA in scoring (34.5), total points (2,831), total rebounds (1,155), field goals made (1,095), free throws attempted (796), and minutes played (3,539), while also averaging 14.1 rebounds, 2.2 assists, 1.1 steals, and 2.1 blocked shots while shooting 51.2 percent from the field and 80.5 percent from the free throw line during the 1974–75 season. Who is it?
Answer on page 78.

38. In what season was Wilt Chamberlain the scoring leader, Bill Russell the rebound leader, and Oscar Robertson the assist leader?
Answer on page 78.

39. Which NBA players surpassed the league's triple-double record of two during his first *week* in the NBA?
Answer on page 78.

40. Which player set an NBA record by shooting 72.7 percent from the field during the 1972–73 season?
Answer on page 78.

41. Which NBA player retired in 2003 because of kidney disease, underwent a kidney transplant in 2004, then returned to play for the Miami Heat in 2005, helping them to the NBA championship in 2006?
Answer on page 78.

42. Who was the player who surpassed Kareem Abdul-Jabbar's record for most games played?
Answer on page 78.

43. Who was the first NBA player to have consecutive 50-point games in the 2000s?
Answer on page 78.

44. Who was the starting center for the Boston Celtics before Bill Russell arrived onto the scene in 1956?
Answer on page 78–79.

45. Which player has scored the most points in a loss? How many points did he score?
Answer on page 79.

46. Who led the NBA in scoring in its first-ever season of 1946–47?
A. George Mikan
B. Max Zaslofsky
C. Joe Fulks
D. Paul Arizin
Answer on page 79.

47. Who led the NBA in scoring at the end of its second season, in 1947–48?
Answer on page 79.

48. While we know Michael Jordan was a dominant scorer, he did not live outside like today's shooters. With that said, what was MJ's highest 3-point attempts per game for a single season?
A. 2.3 attempts per game
B. 3.6 attempts per game
C. 4.5 attempts per game
D. 5.7 attempts per game
Answer on page 79.

PLAYERS

ANSWERS

1. 1-D, 2-E, 3-A, 4-B, 5-C

2. Ray Allen hit 269 three-pointers during the 2005–06 season. That record was broken by Stephen Curry in 2012–13 (272), then in 2014–15 (286), and again in 2015–16 (402).

3.

Chucky Brown (1990–2002)	Jim Jackson (1993–2006)
1989–90 to 1991–92: Cleveland Cavaliers	1992–93 to 1996–97: Dallas Mavericks
1991–92: Los Angeles Lakers	1996–97: New Jersey Nets
1992–93: New Jersey Nets	1997–98: Philadelphia 76ers
1993–94: Dallas Mavericks	1997–98: Golden State Warriors
1994–95 to 1995–96: Houston Rockets	1998–99: Portland Trail Blazers
1996–97: Phoenix Suns	1999–2000 to 2000–01: Atlanta Hawks
1996–97: Milwaukee Bucks	2000–01: Cleveland Cavaliers
1997–98: Atlanta Hawks	2001–02: Miami Heat
1998–99: Charlotte Hornets	2002–03: Sacramento Kings
1999–2000: San Antonio Spurs	2003–04 to 2004–05: Houston Rockets
1999–2000: Charlotte Hornets	2004–05 to 2005–06: Phoenix Suns
2000–01: Golden State Warriors	2005–06: Los Angeles Lakers
2000–01: Cleveland Cavaliers	
2001–02: Sacramento Kings	
(Played for Hornets and Cavaliers twice)	

Tony Massenburg (1991–2005)	Joe Smith (1996–2011)
1990–91 to 1991–92: San Antonio Spurs	1995–96 to 1997–98: Golden State Warriors
1991–92: Charlotte Hornets	1997–98: Philadelphia 76ers
1991–92: Boston Celtics	1998–99 to 1999–2000: Minnesota Timberwolves
1991–92: Golden State Warriors	
1994–95: Los Angeles Clippers	2000–01: Detroit Pistons
1995–96: Toronto Raptors	2001–02 to 2002–03: Minnesota Timberwolves
1995–96: Philadelphia 76ers	
1996–97: New Jersey Nets	2003–04 to 2005–06: Milwaukee Bucks
1997–98 to 1998–99: Vancouver Grizzlies	2006–07: Denver Nuggets
1999–2000: Houston Rockets	2006–07: Philadelphia 76ers
2000–01 to 2001–02: Vancouver/ Memphis Grizzlies	2007–08: Chicago Bulls
	2007–08: Cleveland Cavaliers
2002–03: Utah Jazz	2008–09: Oklahoma City Thunder
2003–04: Sacramento Kings	2008–09: Cleveland Cavaliers
2004–05: San Antonio Spurs	2009–10: Atlanta Hawks
(Played for Spurs and Grizzlies twice)	2010–11: New Jersey Nets
	2010–11: Los Angeles Lakers
	(Played for Timberwolves, 76ers, and Cavaliers twice)

4. Steve Nash had 7,778 assists from 2000 to 2010, just 25 more than runner-up Jason Kidd. (A)

5. You'd think it'd be close, but it's not. While Bill Russell had an incredible 193 games in which he scored at least 20 points and pulled down 20 rebounds, the king is of course Wilt Chamberlain, who had an astounding 566 games where he accomplished such a feat. (C)

6. He didn't get the nickname "Magic" for nothing, as Johnson had 13 instances where he logged at least 20 points and 20 assists. (D)

7. While Westbrook was the first player since "The Big O" to average a triple-double for an entire season, when he did it in back-to-back campaigns (2016–17 and 2017–18), he still has a ways to go before catching Oscar Robertson, who had 174 career triple-doubles. (A)

8. Who says size matters? Definitely not the 5-foot-3 Muggsy Bogues, who averaged 10.7 assists and 1.8 turnovers a game during the 1989–90 season. (C)

9. Wilt the Stilt does it again, as on February 2, 1968, Chamberlain scored 22 points to go along with 25 rebounds and 21 assists. You can guess that his 76ers won that game, defeating the Detriot Pistons, 131–121. (C)

10. If you guessed Elmore Smith, you would be correct. On October 28, 1973, Smith swatted 17 shots to go along with 12 points and 16 rebounds. Truly an outstanding performance. (He also led the league in blocks that season, averaging 4.9 a game.)

The only thing as impressive is that Shaquille O'Neal had 15 blocks in a game (November 20, 1993) while adding 24 points and an astounding 28 rebounds. (D)

11. The record stands with the Spaniard José Calderon, who hit an incredible 151 of 154 free throws during the 2008–09 season for a .9805 percentage. (B)

12. An impressive group of players, but only two are in such an illustrious caterogy. They are:
LeBron James: 2009–10; 29.7 PPG, 8.6 APG, 7.3 RPG
Russell Westbrook: 2016–17; 31.1 PPG, 10.4 APG, 10.7 RPG (D and G)

13. While Isiah Thomas had three such games and Dwyane Wade four, the winner by a resounding number is Russell Westbrook, who has had eight games with 10 or more turnovers for his career. (C)

14. On February 24, 1978, Detroit Pistons point guard Kevin Porter dished 29 assists during a game against the New Jersey Nets. (C)

15. Kobe Bryant had 33,643 points in his career, which is third on the all-time list (and tops for those coming straight from high school). Behind him is LeBron James who, through the 2018–19 season, has 32,543 points.

16. There are only three instances where Kobe was held scoreless when listed as a starter. However, these were not for lack of effort.

On April 1, 2001, against the New York Knicks, Kobe went 0-for-4 in 11 minutes before leaving the game. He had missed the previous five games due to an injured left ankle, which kept him out for the remainder of the game.

On March 5, 2004, against the Seattle SuperSonics, Kobe played only a single minute before injuring his shoulder (which had been operated on the previous offseason) during a collision with Reggie Evans.

On March 15, 2013, against the Indiana Pacers, Kobe went 0-for-4 in 12 minutes before leaving the game. He had sprained his left ankle two nights earlier and, after much discomfort, left the game after the first quarter. (C)

17. In their 18 regular-season matchups, Magic's Lakers beat Bird's Celtics 11 times. In their 19 playoff matchups, Magic's Lakers beat Bird's Celtics . . . 11 times.

18. José Calderon has worn No. 81 for the Cleveland Cavaliers (2017–18) and Detroit Pistons (2018–19) (D)

19. Elvin Hayes grabbed 16,279 rebounds during a pro career that spanned from 1968 to 1981. (B)

20. John Stockton compiled 3,265 steals during a career that spanned from 1984 to 2003. (A)

21. Alvin Robertson, then of the San Antonio Spurs, compiled 301 steals during the 1985–86 season. He is the only player to finish in the top 10 single-season leaders in steals eight times. (B)

22. False. James was second to Oklahoma City Thunder guard Russell Westbrook, who attempted a league-high 1,687 shots.

23. Steve Kerr shot .454 on threes for his career, which spanned from 1988 to 2003. (C)

24. Artis Gilmore shot .599 from the field during a playing career that began in the ABA in 1972 and ended in the NBA in 1988. (A)

25. Jae Crowder has worn No. 99 for the Boston Celtics (2015–17), Cleveland Cavaliers (2017–18), and Utah Jazz (2018–present).

26. James Harden of the Houston Rockets made 265 threes during the 2017–18 season. Paul George of the Oklahoma City Thunder was second with 244.

27. Chamberlain's record was set against the Bill Russell–led Boston Celtics.

28. For the 1951–52 season, Bobby Wanzer of the Rochester Royals shot 90.4 percent (377-for-417) from the free throw line.

29. To no one's surprise, the answer is Wilt Chamberlain, who averaged 37.6 points *as a rookie* for Philadelphia in 1959–60. He would also do so for the next six seasons.

30. Elmore Smith of the Los Angeles Lakers, who had 393 blocks for the season, with an average of 4.9 per game (which also led the league).

31. Oscar Robertson of the Cincinnati Royals, who averaged 11.4 assists during the 1961–62 season.

32. That would be Charlie "Helicopter" Hentz of the Pittsburgh Condors, doing so against the Carolina Cougars in a 1970 game played in Raleigh.

33. An obvious one, as the answer is Rasheed Wallace with 29. The second most is DeMarcus Cousins, who has 14 (thus far) in his career.

34. And again, the answer is Rasheed Wallace, who picked up 41 technical fouls during the 2000–01 season.

35. Though first tested at the college level in 1945, it did not become popular until the ABA included it during their inaugural 1967–68 season. While the ABA would merge with the NBA in 1976, the league would not adopt the shot until the 1979–80 season. With that said, the first NBA player to hit a three-pointer would be Chris Ford of the Boston Celtics, who did so on October 12, 1979.

36. In the 1972–73 season, Nate "Tiny" Archibald of the Kansas City-Omaha Kings led the league with 34.0 points and 11.4 assists. In addition, he also led the league in minutes played with 46.0.

37. That would be Bob McAdoo, who accomplished this incredible feat as a member of the Buffalo Braves.

38. In the 1963–64 season, Chamberlain averaged 34.7 PPG, Russell averaged 24.1 RPG, and Robertson averaged 11.5 APG.

39. The "Big O" strikes again, as it's Oscar Robertson.

40. The answer, again, is Wilt Chamberlain. Another record he can add to his long list of accolades.

41. Alonzo Mourning.

42. On April 6, 1996, Robert Parish played in his 1,561st game, becoming the all-time leader for most games played in a career.

43. On December 3, 2000, Antawn Jamison put up 51 points as a member of the Golden State Warriors against the Los Angeles Lakers. Two nights later, against the Toronto Raptors, Jamison again scored 51 points, becoming the first player to have consecutive 50-point games in the 2000s.

44. For six years before Russell arrived in Boston, the 6-foot-8, 185-pound Ed Macauley was the anchor of the Celtics frontcourt. In fact, he was an All-Star in each of those six seasons with the Celtics. He would play three more seasons (for the St. Louis Hawks) after being traded for Russell, making the All-Star team in 1956–57.

45. On December 8, 1961, the Philadelphia Warriors were beaten by the Los Angeles Lakers, 151–147. While Elgin Baylor had an incredible game for the Lakers, scoring 63 points with 31 rebounds, Wilt Chamberlain stole the show. While his team lost, Chamberlain put up 78 points and 43 rebounds, the former being the most points scored by a single player in a loss.

46. The 6-foot-5 Joe Fulks averaged 23.2 points for the Philadelphia Warriors. Fulks was shot and killed by the son of his girlfriend in 1976. He was just 54 years old. (C)

47. Joe Fulks of the Philadelphia Warriors was the NBA's scoring leader in each of the league's first two seasons. In his second season, Fulks averaged 22.1 points per game. As an aside, he averaged 26.0 points per game the next season and did *not* lead the league in scoring. (That honor went to Minneapolis Lakers center George Mikan, who averaged 28.3 points per game.)

48. In the 1996–97 season, Michael Jordan averaged 29.6 points, 5.9 rebounds, and 4.3 assists per game. However, he only averaged 3.6 three-point attempts per game, which was a career high. For comparison, in 2018–19, James Harden averaged 13.2 three-point attempts per game. Think things have changed a little? (B)

COACHES

QUESTIONS

Coaching in the NBA is a lot like working as a foreman on an assembly line. Everyone there already knows how to play. Your job is to make sure the players understand and perform their roles and work as a unit. You manage personalities, try to keep the peace in the locker room and on the sideline, and attempt to command huddles that consist of no less than 12 people in shorts and high tops whose salaries are likely bigger than your own.

For a college coach, things are a bit different. You have total control over who plays and actual strategy plays a much bigger role. You are the first and last voice of the entire program. You decide who to recruit, who to bench and who will take the most shots.

In the NBA, the general manager makes the majority of the key roster decisions. The coach is usually stuck with what he has. Sometimes, he is blessed with a superstar. Sometimes, he is cursed with a star who doesn't like him. Sometimes, he can get his message across and take an undermanned to the second round of the playoffs. And sometimes, for a coach, that is the greatest reward of all.

Here is a look at some of the best at the biggest levels throughout history. See how much you know.

1. Which coach has the most wins in NBA history?
   A. Lenny Wilkens
   B. Jerry Sloan
   C. Don Nelson
   D. Phil Jackson
   Answer on page 89.

2. Can you name the coach that has the fourth-highest playoff winning percentage, yet a losing regular-season record?
   Answer on page 89.

3. Three coaches have won the NBA Coach of the Year Award three times. Who is the only coach to have won all three with the same team? Who is the only coach to have won all three with different teams?
   Answer on page 89.

4. Who is the third coach to accomplish this feat?
   Answer on page 89.

5. Who was first coach to win NBA titles with multiple teams?
   Answer on page 89.

6. Of those who have coached a minimum of 200 games, who has all-time worst winning percentage?
   Answer on page 89.

7. Who was the first coach inducted into the Naismith Memorial Hall of Fame?
   Answer on page 90.

8. Only one person has coached in more than than 300 playoff games. Who is it?
   Answer on page 90.

9. Aside from the coach above, only three others have coached in more than 200 playoff games. Can you name them?
   Answer on page 90.

10. Which former player has the highest winning percentage as a coach?
    Answer on page 90.

11. Who was the first coach of the New York Knickerbockers?
Answer on page 90.

12. Who was the last coach to win Coach of the Year after having a losing season the year before?
Answer on page 90.

13. Through the 2018–19 season, there are nine head coaches who have won 1,000+ games in their career. Of those nine, only two have never been named Coach of the Year. Who are they?
Answer on page 90.

14. Of the 26 coaches who have been a head coach for 15+ seasons, which has the lowest winning percentage?
Answer on page 91.

15. Only five coaches have managed more than 2,000 games. Who are they?
Answer on page 91.

16. Who is the only man to coach a team to both an NCAA and NBA title?
A. John Wooden
B. Rick Pitino
C. Larry Brown
D. John Calipari
Answer on page 91.

17. Who was the first coach in NBA history whose team finished with a below-.500 record but was still named Coach of the Year?
Answer on page 91.

18. Four coaches have over 1,000 losses for their career. Can you name them?
Answer on page 91.

19. Who was the first African American head coach in the NBA, and all of professional sports?
Answer on page 91.

20. Which two Los Angeles Lakers coaches were drafted by the San Diego Rockets?
A. Pat Riley and Rudy Tomjanovich
B. Mike Dunleavy and Bill Sharman
C. Mike Dunleavy and Rudy Tomjanovich
D. Pat Riley and Mike Brown
Answer on page 91.

21. Which active coach has the most career regular-season victories?
A. Rick Carlisle
B. Mike D'Antoni
C. Gregg Popovich
D. Doc Rivers
Answer on page 91.

22. What about the second-most wins?
Answer on page 91.

23. Which head coach has the lowest playoff winning percentage of those that have won a championship?
A. Jack Ramsay
B. Dick Motta
C. Lenny Wilkens
D. Edward Gottlieb
Answer on page 91.

24. Who is the only coach to win a championship in three professional leagues?
Answer on page 91–92.

25. Who won the ABA Coach of the Year Award in 1971–72 despite leading his team to a totally average 42–42 record?
Answer on page 92.

26. What point guard started with the Philadelphia Warriors, then later led the Golden State Warriors to a championship as their coach?
Answer on page 92.

27. Who is the youngest player-coach in NBA history?
Answer on page 92.

28. Which former NBA great was the first coach of the Buffalo Braves? Hint, his son also played in the NBA.
Answer on page 92.

29. Which of the following had the least amount of wins in their first year as rookie head coach, yet led their team to an NBA championship?
A. Paul Westhead
B. George Senesky
C. Nick Nurse
D. Tyronn Lue
E. Steve Kerr
F. Pat Riley
Answer on page 92.

30. Who was the first woman to win WNBA Coach of the Year?
Answer on page 92–93.

31. Who was the first coach to lead the Kings to the playoffs after the team moved to Sacramento in 1985–86?
Answer on page 93.

32. K. C. Jones led both the Washington Bullets (1978) and Boston Celtics (1984 and 1986) to NBA titles as a coach. But which team did he coach in the ABA?
A. Spirits of St. Louis
B. San Diego Conquistadors
C. New York Nets
D. Kentucky Colonels
Answer on page 93.

33. Who coached the Detroit Pistons to a 30–52 record in 1978–79 before getting fired 12 games into the next season and immediately moving to a career in broadcasting?
Answer on page 93.

34. What current NBA broadcast analyst coached the Kentucky Colonels during the final two seasons of the ABA (1974–76)?
Answer on page 93.

35. Which team fired Chuck Daly before he became head coach of the Detroit Pistons?
Answer on page 93.

36. Which team did Chuck Daly later coach after leading the Detroit Pistons to back-to-back titles in 1989 and '90?
Answer on page 93.

37. Who was the first NBA Hall of Famer to be named WNBA Coach of the Year?
Answer on page 93.

38. Bill Fitch began as an NBA coach with the expansion Cleveland Cavaliers in 1970, then later led two teams to the Finals. Name those teams.
Answer on page 94.

39. Which legendary coach played for Bill Fitch at the University of North Dakota?
Answer on page 94.

40. Phil Jackson, George Karl, and Jerry Sloan are among those to have coached in the old Continental Basketball Association, once considered the NBA's developmental league. Name the only former CBA coach who was an active NBA coach as of the 2018–19 season.
Answer on page 94.

41. What current NBA coach was a member of the Boston Celtics' 1986 title-winning team?
Answer on page 94.

42. Which two head coaches have led the most teams in league history?
Answer on page 94–95.

43. Who was Hall of Fame point guard Jason Kidd's first NBA head coach?
A. George Karl
B. Bill Fitch
C. Don Nelson
D. Dick Motta
Answer on page 95.

44. True or False. Lou Carnesecca never coached a professional team?
Answer on page 95.

COACHES

ANSWERS

1. With 1,335 wins, Don Nelson has more than any other coach in NBA history—three more than second-place Lenny Wilkens. (C)

2. Paul Westhead has the four-highest playoff winning percentage at .684, yet his regular-season record was 183–224 (.450).

3. Gregg Popovich is the only coach to be named NBA Coach of the Year three times with the same team, doing so with the San Antonio Spurs in 2002–03, 2011–12, and 2013–14.
   Pat Riley is the only coach to be named NBA Coach of the Year three times with different teams, doing so with the Los Angeles Lakers (1989–90), New York Knicks (1992–93), and Miami Heat (1996–97).

4. Aside from Pop and Riley, Don Nelson is only the third coach to win the award three times, doing so in 1982–83, 1983–84 (both with the Milwaukee Bucks), and 1991–92 (with the Golden State Warriors).

5. Alex Hannum won a championship with the 1958 St. Louis Hawks, and then in 1967 with the Philadelphia 76ers. Two years later he would win a championship with the ABA's Oakland Oaks.

6. Coaching from 1993 to 2003, Sidney Lowe has the lowest winning percentage at .257 (79–228).

7. There are multiple answers to this question:

- In the inaugural HOF class of 1959, college coaches Walter Meanwell, Henry Clifford "Doc" Carlson, and Phog Allen were inducted.
- If you want to get technical, George Mikan was in the inaugural HOF class and coached the Minneapolis Lakers during the 1957–58 season (to a 9–30 record), but his induction was as a player.
- The first coach with professional experience was Ken Loeffler, who led the BAA's St. Louis Bombers (1946–47 and 1947–48) and Providence Steamrollers (1948–49). However, he was mainly known as a collegiate coach, spending 16 years heading up Yale (1935–36 to 1941–42), Denver (1945–46), La Salle (1949–50 to 1954–55), and Texas A&M (1955–56 to 1956–57).
- The first coach that was elected to the HOF who *only* coached professionally, if we're getting specific, was Red Auerbach, who was inducted in 1969.

8. The Zen Master, Phil Jackson, coached in 333 playoff games, to go along with 11 rings (plus an additional two as a player).

9. Gregg Popovich (284), Pat Riley (282), and Jerry Sloan (202).

10. Through the 2018–19 season, Steve Kerr has a .785 winning percentage as a coach (322–88).

11. Neil Cohalan, who also holds the distinction of winning the first-ever NBA game in 1946–47.

12. After having a 38–44 record for the 2013–14 season, Mike Budenholzer turned the Atlanta Hawks around, leading them to a 60–22 record and all the way to the Eastern Conference finals.

13. Jerry Sloan, who has 1,221 wins (third all time), and Rick Adelman, who has 1,042 wins (ninth all time).

14. In 15 seasons, Byron Scott has a .412 winning percentage:
New Jersey Nets (2000–01 to 2003–04): 149–139 (.517)
New Orleans Hornets/Oklahoma City Hornets-Thunder
 (2004–05 to 2009–10): 203–216 (.484)
Cleveland Cavaliers (2010–11 to 2012–13): 64–166 (.278)
Los Angeles Lakers (2014–15 to 2015–16): 38–126 (.232)

15. Lenny Wilkens (2,487), Don Nelson (2,398), Bill Fitch (2,050), Jerry Sloan (2,024), and Larry Brown (2,002).

16. Larry Brown coached Kansas to a title in 1988 and the Detroit Pistons to a championship in 2004. (C)

17. That would be Johnny "Red" Kerr, who led the expansion Chicago Bulls to a 33–48 record in the 1966–67 season.

18. Lenny Wilkens (1970–2005; 1,332–1,155), Bill Fitch (1971–98; 944–1,106), Don Nelson (1977–2010; 1,335–1,063), and Dick Motta (1968–97; 935–1,017).

19. Bill Russell, who served as player-coach for the Boston Celtics in 1967–68 and 1968–69, winning NBA titles in both seasons.

20. Pat Riley was selected by the Rockets in the 11th round of the 1967 draft. Tomjanovich was selected by the Rockets with the No. 2 overall pick in 1970. (A)

21. Gregg Popovich leads all active coaches with 1,245 victories. (C)

22. Doc Rivers is second on the active list with 894 victories.

23. With a .431 playoff winning percentage, Jack Ramsay has the lowest of any coach that has won an NBA championship. (A)

24. Bill Sharman, who won an ABA title as coach of the Utah Stars in 1971 and an NBA title as coach of the Los Angeles Lakers in 1972. Before that, Sharman won a championship with the Cleveland Pipers of the American

Basketball League (ABL) in 1962. In the event you aren't as familiar with the ABL, just know it was the first pro league to institute a three-point arc.

25. Tom Nissalke of the Dallas Chaparrals. Not only did the Chaparrals finish .500, but were swept in the first round of the playoffs (by the Utah Stars). For his efforts, Nissalke earned a job the following season as coach of the Seattle SuperSonics in the more prestigious NBA. He was not named Coach of the Year that season. Instead, Nissalke was fired before it ended, as the Sonics won just 13 of their first 45 games.

26. Al Attles, who coached Golden State to the 1975 championship with a sweep of the Washington Bullets. As an aside, Attles is the only head coach in NBA history who attended North Carolina A&T.

27. Dave DeBusschere, who at the age of 24 took the role as player-coach with the Detroit Pistons early in the 1964–65 season, leading them the rest of the way and to a 31–49 record (29–40 while as their coach).

28. Dolph Schayes (father of Danny Schayes), who coached the Braves to a 22–60 record in 1970–71. The following season, he coached the Braves to an 0–1 record before being fired.

29. After taking over a 30–11 Cleveland Cavaliers team midway through the 2015–16 season, Tyronn Lue won 27 games while leading his team to an NBA championship, which is the fewest by a rookie head coach in league history. (D)
   The others, in order, are:
> George Senesky (45 wins with the 1955–56 Philadelphia Warriors)
> Paul Westhead (50 wins with the 1979–80 Los Angeles Lakers)
> Pat Riley (50 wins with the 1981–82 Los Angeles Lakers)
> Nick Nurse (58 wins with the 2018–19 Toronto Raptors)
> Steve Kerr (67 wins with the 2014–15 Golden State Warriors)

30. In only her first year at the helm, Marianne Stanley led the Washington Mystics to a 17–15 record—the first winning season in franchise history—while becoming the first female coach to win WNBA Coach of the Year honors.

31. Phil Johnson, who led the Kings to a 37–45 record and the postseason during their first year in Sacramento. It was all downhill for Johnson from there, though. The Kings were swept by the Houston Rockets in the first round, and Johnson was fired the next season after the Kings won just 14 of their first 46 games.

32. After a nine-year playing career with the Boston Celtics, K. C. Jones became head coach of the ABA's San Diego Conquistadors for the 1972–73 season, and finished 30–52. He went on to coach for 17 seasons in the NBA—10 as a head coach and 11 with his Celtics (six as an assistant and five as head coach, leading the team to championships in 1984 and 1986. (B)

33. It's an awesome question, baby! That's right, Hall of Fame college basketball analyst Dick Vitale spent four successful seasons as the head coach at the University of Detroit (now known as Detroit Mercy) before a forgettable two years in the NBA.

34. That would be Hubie Brown, who would coach another 13 years in the NBA with the Atlanta Hawks, New York Knicks, and Memphis Grizzlies.

35. In his first NBA head coaching job, Chuck Daly became the third of four coaches to lead the Cleveland Cavaliers during the 1981–82 season. The Cavs would finish the season 15–67, while Daly's record with the team was 9–32.

36. After nine seasons with the Detroit Pistons, Chuck Daly became head coach of the New Jersey Nets for two seasons.

37. Pistons legend and Hall of Famer Bill Laimbeer led the Detroit Shock to the 2003 WNBA Finals, winning over the Los Angeles Sparks. The Shock would later move to Tulsa (as the Shock) and then find their current home in Dallas (now as the Wings).

38. After nine seasons at the helm of the Cavaliers, Bill Fitch led the Boston Celtics (1981) and Houston Rockets (1986) to the NBA Finals. Interestingly, Fitch's Celtics beat the Rockets for the title in '81, while his Rockets lost to the Celtics in '86. Fitch also coached the New Jersey Nets and Los Angeles Clippers before retiring in 1998.

39. Phil Jackson, who owns the NBA coaching record with 11 championships.

40. Terry Stotts of the Portland Trail Blazers. Stotts was George Karl's assistant with the CBA's Albany Patroons before coaching the Fort Wayne Fury for one season (1991–92).

41. Rick Carlisle, who went on to coach the Detroit Pistons (2001–02 to 2002–03) and Indiana Pacers (2003–04 to 2006–07) before being hired by the Dallas Mavericks in 2008 (where he still coaches the team through the 2018–19 season).

42. Larry Brown has been the head coach of more teams than any other in NBA history, with nine different organizations. However, if you want to include the ABA, he has been with 10.

> 1972–73 to 1973–74: Carolina Cougars (ABA)
> 1974–75 to 1975–76: Denver Nuggets (ABA)
> 1976–77 to 1978–79: Denver Nuggets (NBA)
> 1981–82 to 1982–83: New Jersey Nets
> 1988–89 to 1991–92: San Antonio Spurs
> 1991–92 to 1992–93: Los Angeles Clippers
> 1993–94 to 1996–97: Indiana Pacers
> 1997–98 to 2002–03: Philadelphia 76ers
> 2003–04 to 2004–05: Detroit Pistons
> 2005–06: New York Knicks
> 2008–09 to 2010–11: Charlotte Bobcats

The second is George Karl, who was the head coach for six different organizations:

     1984–85 to 1985–86: Cleveland Cavaliers
     1986–87 to 1978–88: Golden State Warriors
     1991–92 to 1997–98: Seattle SuperSonics
     1998–99 to 2002–03: Milwaukee Bucks
     2004–05 to 2012–13: Denver Nuggets
     2014–15 to 2015–16: Sacramento Kings

43. Over a 19-year career, Jason Kidd played under nine different coaches. However, his first NBA head coach was Dick Motta, who coached Kidd in his first two seasons with the Dallas Mavericks. (D)

44. False. Lou Carnesecca coached the New York Nets from 1970 to 1973.

TEAMS

QUESTIONS

Teamwork. It's the only thing that wins big in the NBA. Yes, individual greatness counts for a lot, but even Michael Jordan didn't become a major winner until Chicago Bulls coach Phil Jackson convinced Jordan that he couldn't do it alone.

And even LeBron James didn't find pro basketball paradise until he teamed up with Dwyane Wade and Chris Bosh with the Miami Heat, then later Kyrie Irving and Kevin Love with the Cleveland Cavaliers.

Those are just two examples. Other teams overachieve just by moving the ball and playing unselfishly on offense, and bending their knees and shuffling their feet on defense.

So as well-known as superstars have become, the NBA truly is all about team. It's every coach's dream to have an entire roster of players fitting together and functioning as one. When it happens, it's a basketball sight to behold.

Of course, when it goes the other way . . . well, things can be just as memorable. Or forgettable, depending on your rooting interest.

Here are some questions on the best and worst, and everywhere in between, when it comes to record-setting teams.

1. Match the team with the city it originally played in:
   1. Philadelphia 76ers   A. Rochester
   2. Houston Rockets   B. Buffalo
   3. Washington Wizards   C. Chicago
   4. Los Angeles Clippers   D. San Diego
   5. Sacramento Kings   E. Syracuse
   Answer on page 111.

2. The Lakers have played the Celtics a total of 290 times in the regular season. But who has the advantage? Which team has won more games in this rivalry?
Answer on page 111.

3. Through the 2018–19 season, which team has the best overall winning percentage?
Answer on page 111.

4. Through the 2018–19 season, which team has the worst overall winning percentage?
Answer on page 111.

5. Which of these franchises eventually became the Los Angeles Clippers?
A. San Diego Conquistadors
B. Buffalo Braves
C. Chicago Stags
D. Providence Steamrollers
Answer on page 111.

6. Which of these franchises eventually became the Atlanta Hawks?
A. Buffalo Bisons
B. Chicago Zephrys
C. St. Louis Bombers
D. Kentucky Colonels
Answer on page 111.

7. Only four teams have nicknames that do not end with the letter "s." Name them.
Answer on page 111.

8. Which team was the first to have both a 10-game winning streak and a 10-game losing streak in the same season?
Answer on page 111.

9. The Boston Celtics went 40–1 at the Boston Garden during the 1985–86 regular season. Name the only team to defeat the Celtics on their home hardwood.
Answer on page 112.

10. What NBA team failed to make the playoffs in 1994 for the first time since 1976?
Answer on page 112.

11. Only two teams won two titles in the 1970s. Who were they?
Answer on page 112.

12. Which team scored the least amount of points in a single game since the 24-second shot clock was introduced?
Answer on page 112.

13. The Golden State Warriors broke the Chicago Bulls' record for most single-season wins with 73 in 2015–16 (Chicago won 72 games in 1995–96). The Bulls bettered the mark of 69, set by the 1971–72 Lakers. Whose record did those Lakers beat?
Answer on page 112.

14. Which NBA team was the first to average more than 100 points per game for an entire season?
Answer on page 112.

15. Who was the first coach in Dallas Mavericks history?
A. John MacLeod
B. Don Nelson
C. Dick Motta
D. Hank Iba
Answer on page 112.

16. Which 2012–13 team ended up being the oldest in NBA history (through the 2018–19 season)?
A. Denver Nuggets
B. New York Knicks
C. Dallas Mavericks
D. Sacramento Kings
Answer on page 112.

17. In what year did the San Antonio Spurs have a player lead the league in field goal percentage and another player lead the league in three-point field goal percentage?
Answer on page 112.

18. Which member of the Washington Bullets' 1978 championship team became the franchise's coach in 1987?
Answer on page 113.

19. What were the Brooklyn Nets called as one of the ABA's charter franchises in 1967–68?
Answer on page 113.

20. The Texas Chaparrals were an ABA franchise in 1971. They eventually went by another nickname and are now in the NBA. Name them.
Answer on page 113.

21. Which team did the 1962 expansion Chicago Packers eventually become?
Answer on page 113.

22. Which NBA franchise folded after just one season in 1950, but re-emerged seventeen years later as a new franchise and remains in the NBA today?
Answer on page 113.

23. Only one ABA franchise was named after an original NBA team . . . but changed their name to the Virginia Squires after just one ABA season. Can you name them?
Answer on page 113.

24. Who is the Philadelphia 76ers's all-time leader in assists?
A. Julius Erving
B. Eric Snow
C. Allen Iverson
D. Maurice Cheeks
Answer on page 113.

25. Who is the Minneapolis Lakers's all-time leader in points?
A. Elgin Baylor
B. George Mikan
C. Whitey Skoog
D. Jerry West
Answer on page 113.

26. Who is the New Orleans Jazz's all-time leader in points?
A. Pete Maravich
B. Gail Goodrich
C. Otto Moore
D. Aaron James
Answer on page 113–114.

27. Who is the Seattle SuperSonics's all-time leader in points?
A. Shawn Kemp
B. Fred Brown
C. Xavier McDaniel
D. Gary Payton
Answer on page 114.

28. Who is the Phoenix Suns's all-time leading scorer?
    A. Kevin Johnson
    B. Amar'e Stoudemire
    C. Walter Davis
    D. Steve Nash
    Answer on page 114.

29. Who holds the Kings's record for points scored since the team moved to Sacramento 1985?
    A. Mitch Richmond
    B. DeMarcus Cousins
    C. Chris Webber
    D. Peja Stojaković
    Answer on page 114.

30. Who holds the Dallas Mavericks's record for career points per game average with the franchise?
    A. Rolando Blackmon
    B. Mark Aguirre
    C. Dirk Nowitzki
    D. Jamal Mashburn
    Answer on page 114.

31. Who is only the member of the Warriors to lead the team in offensive rebounds in seven separate seasons?
    A. Erick Dampier
    B. Draymond Green
    C. Larry Smith
    D. Danny Fortson
    Answer on page 114.

32. Who snapped the Los Angeles Lakers's NBA-record 33-game winning streak in the 1971–72 season?
    Answer on page 114.

33. Which of the following teams had the highest scoring average in NBA history?
A. 1991–92 Denver Nuggets
B. 1961–62 Philadelphia Warriors
C. 2017–18 Houston Rockets
D. 1978–79 San Antonio Spurs
Answer on page 114.

34. What team holds the record for most points in the first half with 107?
Answer on page 114.

35. Which team holds the record for most points in the first quarter with 51?
Answer on page 115.

36. Which team holds the record for fewest points in the second half?
Answer on page 115.

37. Which team holds the record for most points scored in a third quarter with 57?
Answer on page 115.

38. Which team holds the record for most points scored in a five-minute overtime period?
Answer on page 115.

39. Which two teams combined to score a measly two points in overtime to set a record low?
Answer on page 115.

40. Which franchise won their first and only NBA championship after finishing with a winning record for the first time?
Answer on page 115.

41. In which city did the Atlanta Hawks play 12 "home" games during the 1984–85 season due to sagging attendance in Atlanta?
Answer on page 115.

42. The expansion Milwaukee Bucks held a fan vote in 1968 to name the team. Fans voted for a nickname other than the Bucks, but the team's owner overrode their choice. Can you guess the fans' choice?
Answer on page 115.

43. What was the name of the first NBA team to play home games in Indianapolis?
Answer on page 115.

44. Which NBA team traded superstars Moses Malone and Bob McAdoo in the same season?
Answer on page 116.

45. What NBA team, aside from the Chicago Bulls, has retired Michael Jordan's No. 23 in honor of him?
Answer on page 116.

46. Who is the all-time assists leader for the Orlando Magic?
A. Penny Hardaway
B. Scott Skiles
C. Nick Anderson
D. Jameer Nelson
Answer on page 116.

47. Who is the all-time assists leader for the Houston Rockets?
A. James Harden
B. Calvin Murphy
C. Hakeem Olajuwon
D. Kenny Smith
Answer on page 116.

48. Who is the all-time three-point field goal leader for the Sacramento Kings?

A. Mike Bibby

B. Peja Stojaković

C. Jason Williams

D. Mitch Richmond

Answer on page 116.

49. Who holds the Denver Nuggets's record for career points per game average with the franchise?

A. Alex English

B. Allen Iverson

C. Kiki Vandeweghe

D. Carmelo Anthony

Answer on page 116.

50. Who is the all-time leader in offensive rebounds for the Miami Heat?

A. Alonzo Mourning

B. Rony Seikaly

C. Udonis Haslem

D. P. J. Brown

Answer on page 116.

51. Who is the all-time leader in minutes played for the Bucks?

A. Sidney Moncrief

B. Glenn Robinson

C. Kareem Abdul-Jabbar

D. Bob Dandridge

Answer on page 116.

52. Kevin Garnett is the all-time leader in almost every category for the Minnesota Timberwolves—except three-pointers. So, who is the all-time leader in three-point field goals? What about three-point field goals attempted?
    A. Isaiah Rider
    B. Wally Szczerbiak
    C. Anthony Peeler
    D. Andrew Wiggins
    Answer on page 116.

53. Who has committed the most personal fouls in Pacers history?
    A. Reggie Miller
    B. Dale Davis
    C. Rik Smits
    D. Jeff Foster
    Answer on page 116.

54. Who is the all-time steals leader for the New York Knicks?
    A. Walt Frazier
    B. Mark Jackson
    C. Micheal Ray Richardson
    D. Patrick Ewing
    Answer on page 117.

55. Who is the all-time leader in offensive rebounds for the Grizzlies?
    A. Zach Randolph
    B. Marc Gasol
    C. Pau Gasol
    D. Bryant Reeves
    Answer on page 117.

56. Who is the all-time assists leader for the Washington Bullets/ Wizards?
    A. Earl Monroe
    B. Wes Unseld

C. John Wall
D. Rod Strickland
Answer on page 117.

57. Who is the all-time leader in personal fouls for the Toronto Raptors?
A. Vince Carter
B. Chris Bosh
C. Amir Johnson
D. DeMar DeRozan
Answer on page 117.

58. Who is the all-time leader in games started for the *original* Charlotte Hornets?
A. Larry Johnson
B. Muggsy Bogues
C. David Wesley
D. Glen Rice
Answer on page 117.

59. Who is the all-time leader in offensive rebounds for the Cleveland Cavaliers?
A. LeBron James
B. Larry Nance
C. Brad Daugherty
D. Zydrunas Ilgauskas
Answer on page 117.

60. Who is the all-time steals leader for the Dallas Mavericks?
A. Derek Harper
B. Jason Kidd
C. Brad Davis
D. Dirk Nowitzki
Answer on page 117.

61. While we know that most Utah Jazz records are held by either John Stockton or Karl Malone, what about the all-time leader for blocks? Hint, it's neither Stockton nor Malone.
Answer on page 117.

62. Who is the all-time leader in free throws for the Philadelphia 76ers?
A. Charles Barkley
B. Allen Iverson
C. Hal Greer
D. Dolph Schayes
Answer on page 117.

63. Who is the all-time leader in defensive rebounds for the Phoenix Suns?
A. Amar'e Stoudemire
B. Alvan Adams
C. Shawn Marion
D. Charles Barkley
Answer on page 118.

64. Who is the all-time blocks leader for the Portland Trail Blazers? And to make this question more difficult, we're adding additional options!
A. Bill Walton
B. Arvydas Sabonis
C. Clifford Robinson
D. Rasheed Wallace
E. LaMarcus Aldridge
F. Mychal Thompson
G. Joel Przybilla
Answer on page 118.

65. Who is the all-time leader in games started for the New Jersey Nets?
A. Jason Kidd
B. Kerry Kittles
C. Derek Coleman
D. Buck Williams
Answer on page 118.

66. What about the Brooklyn Nets?
Answer on page 118.

67. Who is the all-time leader in *missed* field goals for the Detroit Pistons?
A. Joe Dumars
B. Dave Bing
C. Bill Laimbeer
D. Isiah Thomas
Answer on page 118.

68. Who is the all-time leader in minutes played for the San Francisco Warriors?
A. Wilt Chamberlain
B. Tom Gola
C. Joe Graboski
D. Paul Arizin
Answer on page 118.

69. Which team had the lowest turnovers per game average for a season?
A. 2011–12 Philadelphia 76ers
B. 2005–06 Detroit Pistons
C. 2016–17 Charlotte Hornets
D. 1995–96 Chicago Bulls
Answer on page 118.

70. Which team had the highest turnovers per game average for a season?

A. 1976–77 Philadelphia 76ers

B. 1972–73 Buffalo Braves

C. 1976–77 Denver Nuggets

D. 1984–85 Seattle SuperSonics

Answer on page 118.

TEAMS

ANSWERS

1. 1-E, 2-B, 3-A, 4-D, 5-C

2. In the 290 matchups between these two rivalries, the Celtics have won 160 (55 percent) while the Lakers have won 130 (45 percent).

3. That would be the San Antonio Spurs, who have a .602 winning percentage. Now, if you're going by *only* their NBA winning percentage, then it would still be the Spurs, with a .622 winning percentage.

4. At .398, the Minnesota Timberwolves have the lowest winning percentage of any current NBA team.

5. The Buffalo Braves played from 1970 to 1978, before moving to San Diego. They became the LA Clippers in 1984. (B)

6. The Buffalo Bisons lasted just 38 games in 1946, before becoming the Tri-Cities Blackhawks from 1946 to 1951; the Milwaukee Hawks from 1951 to 1955; and the St. Louis Hawks from 1955 to 1968 before finding what appears to be a permanent home in Atlanta. (A)

7. The Miami Heat, Orlando Magic, Utah Jazz, and Oklahoma City Thunder.

8. During the 1996–97 season, the Phoenix Suns had both a 10-game winning streak and 10-game losing streak. They finished the season at 40–42.

9. On December 6, 1985, the Portland Trail Blazers defeated the Celtics at Boston Garden, 121–103, being the only team to accomplish that feat for the entire season.

10. After 17 straight seasons of making the playoffs, which included five titles, the Los Angeles Lakers missed the playoffs in the 1993–94 season, finishing with a 33–49 record.

11. The New York Knicks (1969–70 and 1972–73) and Boston Celtics (1973–74 and 1975–76).

12. On April 10, 1999, the Miami Heat defeated the Chicago Bulls, 82–49. The highest point total in a quarter for the Bulls was 16 in the fourth, while the lowest was eight in the first. The Bulls's leading scorer, Kornel David, finished with 13 points.

13. The 1966–67 Philadelphia 76ers went 68–13 during the regular season and defeated the San Francisco Warriors in the NBA Finals.

14. The 1954–55 Boston Celtics averaged 101.3 PPG.

15. Dick Motta coached the Mavericks from 1980 to 1987. He returned in 1994 to coach the team for two more seasons. (C)

16. The New York Knicks in 2012–13 had an average age of 32 years and 240 days old—thanks to the likes of Jason Kidd (40), Marcus Camby (39), Kurt Thomas (39), and rookie Pablo Prigioni (35). Yes, Prigioni was a rookie . . . at 35 years of age. (B)

17. The season was 1982–83, when Spurs center Artis Gilmore shot a league-best .626 from the field and guard Mike Dunleavy shot a league-best .345 from beyond the arc. That same season, shooting guard George Gervin was fourth in free throw percentage at .853, and point guard Johnny Moore was second in assists at 9.8 and third in steals at 2.52.

18. After a 13-year playing career with the Bullets and a season as assistant coach, Wes Unseld coached the Bullets from 1987 to 1994. He had less luck as a coach, going 202–345 (.369) during his seven years at the helm.

19. The New Jersey Americans, though that moniker lasted just one season. They then became the New York Nets, followed by the New Jersey Nets in 1978, followed by the Brooklyn Nets in 2013.

20. You now know them as the San Antonio Spurs.

21. The Packers lasted just the 1961–62 season before becoming the Chicago Zephyrs for the following season. The franchise then became the Baltimore Bullets from 1963 to 1973, before moving to DC to become the Capital Bullets during the 1973–74 season. They were renamed the Washington Bullets and stayed that way until 1997, when their name was changed to the Wizards.

22. The Denver Nuggets, who returned to pro basketball in the ABA as the Denver Rockets before becoming the Nuggets in 1975 and merging into the NBA following the season.

23. That would be the Washington Capitols, who existed in 1970–71 before becoming the Squires. They were also the Oakland Oaks for one year (1968–69) before heading East.

24. Maurice Cheeks passed for 6,212 assists with the Sixers from 1978 to 1989. (D)

25. As Jerry West only played in LA and Elgin Baylor played just two seasons in Minneapolis, the all-time leader is George Mikan with 1,680 points. Fun fact: Mikan was also a member of the Naismith Memorial Hall of Fame's inaugural class in 1959. (B)

26. With 8,034 points, Pete Maravich scored the most points for the Jazz during their short-lived time in New Orleans. Maravich's No. 7

jersey is not only retired by the Jazz, but the New Orleans Pelicans as well, and his No. 44 is retired by the Atlanta Hawks. (A)

27. In the rich history of Seattle basketball, there is one player who has scored more than any other Sonic. Playing on the team from 1991 to 2003, "The Glove" Gary Payton scored 18,207 points—the most in franchise history. In fact, he's also the leader in games played (999), minutes (36,858), field goals (7,292), three-pointers (973), assists (7,384), and steals (2,107). But when you play that long, you also lead in some less flattering categories, as he also led the franchise in turnovers (2,507) and personal fouls (2,577). (D)

28. Walter Davis compiled 15,666 points during a Suns career that spanned from 1977 to 1988. (C)

29. Mitch Richmond scored 12,070 points during a career with the Kings that spanned from 1991 to 1998. (A)

30. Mark Aguirre averaged 24.6 points per game as a member of the Mavericks from 1981 to 1989. (B)

31. Larry Smith, who led the team in 1980–81, 1981–82, 1983–84, 1984–85, 1985–86, 1986–87, and 1988–89, and holds the team record for offensive rebounds in a season, collecting 433 in 1980–81. (C)

32. The Kareem Abdul-Jabbar–led Milwaukee Bucks on January 9, 1972, defeating them, 120–104.

33. The 1991–92 Denver Nuggets averaged an all-time high 126.48 points per game. It got them nowhere, however, as they finished just 24–58. (A)

34. The 1990–91 Phoenix Suns, who scored 107 points on their way to a 173–143 win over the Denver Nuggets on November 10, 1990. Five members of the Suns scored at least 20 points, with Cedric Ceballos coming off the bench to lead the way with 32.

35. The 2018–19 Golden State Warriors, who set the mark in a 142–111 win over the Denver Nuggets on January 15, 2019. The Milwaukee Bucks came within a point of tying the mark with a 50-point first quarter less than a month later.

36. The 2005–06 New Orleans/Oklahoma City Hornets, who bumbled their way to 16 second-half points and a 89–67 loss to the Los Angeles Clippers on March 1, 2006. But at least the Hornets were consistent, scoring eight points in both the third and fourth quarters.

37. That would again be the Golden State Warriors—though this mark was set thirty years earlier in a 155–143 win over the Sacramento Kings on March 4, 1989.

38. The 1996–97 New Jersey Nets, who scored 25 points in OT in a 106–95 win over the Los Angeles Clippers on November 30, 1996.

39. The Denver Nuggets and Charlotte Hornets on January 13, 1997. The Hornets won, 102–100, as Tony Smith's jumper with 1:36 left in OT was the only basket needed. Perhaps fittingly, those were Smith's only two points of the game.

40. The Atlanta Hawks, who were actually the St. Louis Hawks when they accomplished this feat in 1958. Interestingly, the Hawks advanced to the championship series the previous season despite finishing with a losing record.

41. This should be a big, easy question. Yes, the Hawks played 12 games in New Orleans during the 1984–85 season.

43. Fans chose the Robins, named after Wisconsin's state bird.

43. The Olympians, who lasted from 1950 to 1953. They were the Jets for one season before that as a member of the BAA.

44. The Buffalo Braves, who sent Moses Malone to the Houston Rockets on October 24, 1976, then dealt Bob McAdoo to the New York Knicks on December 9, 1976.

45. The Miami Heat, who retired Jordan's number in 2003 prior to his final game in Miami. Jordan was playing for the Washington Wizards at the time.

46. A member of the Magic, from 2004 to 2014, Jameer Nelson collected 3,501 assists, which is 725 more than second-place Scott Skiles. (D)

47. While James Harden is in a close second with 4,201, Calvin Murphy is the current all-time leader with 4,402 assists during his career (all with the Rockets). (B)

48. With 1,070 three-point field goals, Croatian-born Peja Stojaković leads the Kings with Mitch Richmond (993) a close second. (B)

49. Averaging 25.9 points per game, Alex English has the highest PPG average for the Nuggets, just edging out Allen Iverson (25.6). (A)

50. With 101 more offensive boards than Alonzo Mourning (1,505), Udonis Haslem leads the Heat all-time with 1,606. (C)

51. With 22,094 minutes, 40 more than Sidney Moncrief, Bob Dandridge has the most minutes played in the history of the Bucks organization. (D)

52. With 25 more three-pointers made than Kevin Love (440), Anthony Peeler has hit the most treys for the Wolves (465). However, Andrew Wiggins has attempted 65 more than Peeler (1,226) with 1,291. (C, D)

53. With 3,011 personal fouls during his Pacers career, Rik Smits is the all-time leader in franchise history. Reggie Miller is the closest with 2,730. (C)

54. Would you have guessed it was the big guy? That's right, with 1,061 steals—217 more than Charles Oakley (844)—Hall of Fame center Patrick Ewing leads the franchise among all others. You can add this to the fifteen other records he holds for the team. (D)

55. With 1,895 offensive rebounds, Zach Randolph has the most in Grizzlies history. Following him on the list are the Gasol brothers, Marc (1,318) and Pau (1,200). (A)

56. With an impressive 5,282 and counting, John Wall is the all-time assists leader for the Washington franchise. (C)

57. Does one of these choices look different than the others? It should, as Amir Johnson is the all-time leader in personal fouls for the Toronto Raptors with 1,524, which is 25 more than DeMar DeRozan (1,499). (C)

58. Playing from 1989 to 2002 before leaving for New Orleans, the all-time leader in games started for the original Charlotte Hornets is Muggsy Bogues with 501. Behind him is Larry Johnson and David Wesley (both with 372). (B)

59. With 2,336, Zydrunas Ilgauskas has the most offensive rebounds in Cavaliers history. (D)

60. With 1,551 steals—341 more than Dirk Nowitzki (1,210)—Derek Harper is the all-time steals leader for the Dallas Mavericks. (A)

61. Playing all 11 of his NBA seasons with the Utah Jazz, Mark Eaton is the all-time leader in blocks for the franchise with 3,064.

62. With 1,590 more than the second-place Iverson (5,122), Hall of Famer Dolph Schayes made the most free throws in 76ers franchise history with 6,712. (D)

63. Though he leads the franchise in offensive rebounds (2,015) and total rebounds (6,937), the answer is *not* Alvan Adams. He is second behind "The Matrix." That's right, Shawn Marion had 4,927 defensive rebounds as a member of the Phoenix Suns, only five ahead of Adams (4,922). (C)

64. With 768 blocks—42 more than second-place Clifford Robinson (726)—Mychal Thompson is the all-time blocks leader for the Portland Trail Blazers. (F)

65. Playing in New Jersey from 1978–2012, the all-time leaders in games started for these Nets is Buck Williams with 633—129 more than Jason Kidd (504). (D)

66. While starting in 508 games with the Atlanta Hawks before joining the Nets, Joe Johnson is the all-time leader while the team has been in Brooklyn with 216.

67. While he is the franchise leader in numerous categories, including field goals (both made and attempted), free throws (made and attempted), assists, and steals, Isiah Thomas is also the leader in most field goals missed with 8,710. (D)

68. With 24,897 minutes played, Paul Arizin is the all-time leader for the San Francisco Warriors, who were located in that city from 1963 to 1971. (D)

69. Averaging 11.18 turnovers per game, the lowest for any team in a single season, the 2011–12 Philadelphia 76ers hold the league record. The Sixers would finish with a 35–31 record, losing to the Chicago Bulls in the first round of the Eastern Conference playoffs. (A)

70. Averaging 24.52 turnovers per game, the highest for any team in a single season, the 1976–77 Denver Nuggets hold the league record. Amazingly, the Nuggets would go 50–32 for the season, and make it to the Western Conference semifinals before being eliminated by the Portland Trail Blazers. (C)

HALFTIME

MISCELLANY

QUESTIONS

1. Match the player to his nickname (Easy)
   1. The Human Highlight Film   A. Robert Parish
   2. The Dream   B. Ray Allen
   3. Dr. J   C. Dennis Rodman
   4. The Iceman   D. Shawn Marion
   5. Big Country   E. Julius Erving
   6. The Matrix   F. Dominique Wilkins
   7. The Worm   G. Chris Anderson
   8. Birdman   H. Bryant Reeves
   9. The Chief   I. George Gervin
   10. Jesus Shuttlesworth   J. Hakeem Olajuwon
   Answer on page 125.

2. Match the player to his nickname (Hard)
   1. The Houdini of the   A. Billy Cunningham
      Hardwood   B. Lamar Odom
   2. The White Mamba   C. Fred Hoiberg
   3. Skip To My Lou   D. Rafer Alston
   4. Bad News   E. Brian Scalabrine
   5. The Mayor   F. John Salley
   6. The Human Victory Cigar   G. Marvin Barnes
   7. The Candy Man   H. Bob Cousy
   8. Spider   I. Darko Miličić
   9. The Flying Dutchman   J. Rik Smits
   10. Kangaroo Kid
   Answer on page 125.

3. Match the team with their animal mascot:

1. Indiana Pacers	A. Bison
2. Detroit Pistons	B. Condor
3. San Antonio Spurs	C. Bear
4. Oklahoma City Thunder	D. Dragon
5. Houston Rockets	E. Gorilla
6. Phoenix Suns	F. Mountain Lion
7. Denver Nuggets	G. Panther
8. Orlando Magic	H. Horse
9. Los Angeles Clippers	I. Coyote
10. Portland Trail Blazers	J. Mountain Lion

Answer on page 125–126.

4. Which NBA player was called upon and succeeded in saving the life of a dolphin?
   Answer on page 126.

5. In what 1979 basketball movie did Julius Erving star?
   Answer on page 126.

6. Kevin Love's uncle, Mike Love, is a founding member of what band?
   Answer on page 126.

7. What 1979 basketball movie featured NBA player Bernard King, whose school, Cadwallader University, was coached by Gabe Kaplan of *Welcome Back Kotter* fame?
   Answer on page 126.

8. Who were the two baseball Hall of Fame pitchers to play with the Harlem Globetrotters?
   Answer on page 126.

9. Who is the only player to win an NBA championship as well as a World Series?
   Answer on page 126.

10. After the fall of the USSR, the Lithuanian national team could not afford jerseys for the 1992 Olympics. Which rock band stepped up to become the team's financial backers?
Answer on page 127.

11. The 2015–16 Dallas Mavericks had three players on the roster who played the same position and were born on the same day. Who were they?
Answer on page 127.

12. Which former NBA point guard played high school basketball with NFL Hall of Famer Randy Moss?
Answer on page 127.

13. While we all know that Ray Allen starred in Spike Lee's acclaimed film *He Got Game*, can you name the other four NBA players that appeared in the movie?
Answer on page 127.

14. How many months did Larry Bird's Celtics have a losing record during his career?
Answer on page 127.

15. How many movies has Shaquille O'Neal been in? Can you name them?
Answer on page 127.

MISCELLANY

ANSWERS

1. 1-F, 2-J, 3-E,4-I, 5-H, 6-D, 7-C, 8-G, 9-A, 10-B

2. 1-H, 2-E, 3-D, 4-G, 5-C, 6-I, 7-B, 8-F, 9-J, 10-A

3. 1. (G) The Indiana Pacers's mascot, Boomer, was introduced in 1991, and has been nicknamed the "Pacers Panther."

2. (H) The Detroit Pistons's mascot, Hooper, was introduced in 1996, and is a horse (for "horsepower," as Detroit is known as the Motor City.)

3. (I) The San Antonio Spurs's mascot, The Coyote, was introduced in 1983 (and inducted into the Mascot Hall of Fame in 2007).

4. (A) The Oklahoma City Thunder's mascot, Rumble the Bison, was introduced in 2009 and his name derives from the sound of, you guessed it, thunder.

5. (C) The Houston Rockets's mascot, Clutch the Bear, was introduced in 1995 and named after Houston's nickname of "Clutch City." Clutch was inducted into the Mascot Hall of Fame in 2006.

6. (E) The Phoenix Suns's mascot, Go the Gorilla, was introduced in 1980 almost by accident, as a messenger for Eastern Onion, a singing telegram service, was the first to show up in a gorilla costume, which quickly took off. Go the Gorilla would be inducted into the Mascot Hall of Fame in 2005.

7. (J) The Denver Nuggets's mascot, Rocky the Mountain Lion, was introduced in 1990, and was elected into the Mascot Hall of Fame in 2008.

8. (D) The Orlando Magic's mascot, Stuff the Magic Dragon, was

introduced in 1989, and was a play on Puff the Magic Dragon and some-one "stuffing" a basketball. As the team is located in Orlando, the con-nection to Disney World (magic) is obvious. Fun fact: The unofficial mascot of Epcot is Figment the Dragon.

9. (B) The Los Angeles Clippers's mascot, Chuck the Condor, was introduced in 2016, as the condor is the state bird of California.

10. (F) The Portland Trail Blazers's mascot, Blaze the Trail Cat, was introduced in 2002, and is a play on those who "blazed a trail" to the West and the high population of mountain lions in the Oregon parks.

4. Clifford Ray of the Golden State Warriors. In April 1978, Ray received a telephone call from the nearby Marine World aquarium in Redwood City. One of the facility's top attractions, Dr. Spock, had somehow swal-lowed a large metal bolt. Not wanting to risk surgery, veterinarians asked Ray to use his 45-inch arm to reach inside the dolphin's stomach to remove the bolt, which he did on his first attempt. The dolphin seemed to realize what Ray was attempting to do and remained calm throughout the process.

5. *The Fish that Saved Pittsburgh* (1979), which also starred Kareem Abdul-Jabbar (as himself) and Marv Albert (as himself), as well as numerous other NBA stars.

6. Mike Love, along with original members Brian Wilson, Dennis Wil-son, Carl Wilson, and Al Jardine, founded The Beach Boys in 1961.

7. The movie was *Fast Break*.

8. The two baseball Hall of Fame pitchers to play with the Harlem Globetrotters were Bob Gibson and Ferguson Jenkins.

9. Gene Conley won three-consecutive NBA titles as a member of the Boston Celtics in the 1958–59, 1959–60, and 1960–61 seasons, and was a pitcher on the Milwaukee Braves squad that won the 1957 World Series.

10. Not knowing any of the players, The Grateful Dead stepped in to fund the Lithuanian team's jerseys, which were obviously tie-dyed.

11. Deron Williams, Raymond Felton, and J. J. Barea were all point guards for the 2015–16 Mavericks, and all born on June 26, 1984.

12. That would be "White Chocolate," Jason Williams. Both Williams and Moss played for the now-defunct DuPont High School in Belle, West Virginia, leading the team to three state championships. Williams is the only player in school history to reach 1,000 points and 500 assists.

13. Along with Ray Allen, Spike Lee's film *He Got Game* included NBA players Travis Best, Walter McCarty, John Wallace, and Rick Fox.

14. None!

15. The great Shaquille O'Neal has appeared (either as himself, in character, or as a voice actor) in 18 major motion pictures. They are:

Blue Chips (1994)	*Jack and Jill* (2011)
Kazaam (1996)	*Thunderstruck* (2012)
Good Burger (1997)	*Grown Ups 2* (2013)
Steel (1997)	*The Smurfs 2* (2013)
Freddie Got Fingered (2001)	*The Lego Movie* (2014)
The Wash (2001)	*Blended* (2014)
After the Sunset (2004)	*Show Dogs* (2018)
Scary Movie 4 (2006)	*Uncle Drew* (2018)
The House Bunny (2008)	*What Men Want* (2019)

THIRD QUARTER

ALL-STARS

QUESTIONS

The NBA All-Star Game was like most things in the league's formative years—almost as a gimmick to create some buzz and get fans in the door.

It was actually the brainchild of NBA president Maurice Podoloff, public relations man Haskell Cohen, and Boston Celtics owner Walter A. Brown in 1951. Major League Baseball already had an All-Star Game and college basketball was coming off a major point-shaving scandal. Cohen suggested pro basketball could benefit with an exhibition game involving the league's top players, and Brown offered to host and cover all expenses (and potential losses).

Right away, it was a hit, with the first All-Star Game being held in Boston and drawing a crowd of nearly 11,000. At the time, the attendance for most games was just more than 3,000, so the league couldn't have been more thrilled with the turnout for the East's 111–94 win over the West. (It didn't hurt that Celtics big man Ed Macauley was named MVP in front of the home fans.)

The league continued to use the East vs. West format all the way until 2017, when it switched to a vote by team "captains," or the top vote-getter in each conference.

The game has since turned into an entire weekend with dunk, three-point, and overall skills competitions, along with plenty of parties. As originally intended, it's an opportunity for the league to celebrate itself and become the focus of the sports world.

1. In what season was the first NBA All-Star Game played, and who was the MVP?
   Answer on page 139.

2. Name the player that has started the most All Star Games.
   Answer on page 139.

3. Who are the only two teammates to tie for All-Star Game MVP?
   Answer on page 139.

4. Which player has made the most All-Star appearances?
   A. Tim Duncan
   B. Kareem Abdul-Jabbar
   C. Kobe Bryant
   D. Michael Jordan
   Answer on page 139.

5. Who won the first Three-Point Contest?
   Answer on page 139.

6. Who are the only two shooters that have won three Three-Point Contests?
   Answer on page 139.

7. Who won the first Slam Dunk Contest?
   Answer on page 140.

8. Which of the following is a three-time Slam Dunk Contest winner?
   A. Michael Jordan
   B. Dominique Wilkins
   C. Nate Robinson
   D. Vince Carter
   Answer on page 140.

9. Which was the first team to boast both the slam-dunk and three-point champion in the same season?
   Answer on page 140.

10. Who was the first to play 10+ seasons in the NBA with his only All-Star appearance being during his rookie season?
Answer on page 140.

11. Who held the record for most total field goal attempts in All-Star history through the end of the 2018–19 season?
A. Michael Jordan
B. LeBron James
C. George Gervin
D. Kareem Abdul-Jabbar
Answer on page 140.

12. Who holds the record for most made free throws in All-Star Game history?
A. Elgin Baylor
B. Jerry West
C. Kobe Bryant
D. Bob Pettit
Answer on page 140.

13. Who has compiled the most offensive rebounds in All-Star Game history?
A. Shaquille O'Neal
B. Wilt Chamberlain
C. Hakeem Olajuwon
D. Moses Malone
Answer on page 140.

14. Who is second behind Wilt Chamberlain (197) for total rebounds in All-Star play?
A. Bob Pettit
B. Bill Russell
C. Tim Duncan
D. Jerry Lucas
Answer on page 140.

15. Who has compiled the most assists in All-Star Game history?
   A. Chris Paul
   B. Magic Johnson
   C. Isiah Thomas
   D. Jason Kidd
   Answer on page 140.

16. Who has compiled the most steals in All-Star Game history?
   A. Michael Jordan
   B. Dwyane Wade
   C. Kobe Bryant
   D. Allen Iverson
   Answer on page 140.

17. Who has the highest scoring average in All-Star Game history?
   A. Giannis Antetokounmpo
   B. Kevin Durant
   C. Paul George
   D. Paul Westphal
   Answer on page 140.

18. Only three players are perfect from the free throw line in All-Star Games. Clyde Drexler and Gary Payton are two. Who's the third?
   A. Kevin Garnett
   B. Archie Clark
   C. Adrian Dantley
   D. Chet Walker
   Answer on page 141.

19. He was viewed as almost strictly an offensive threat in the 1970s, yet he also averaged the most steals in All-Star Game history. Who is he?
   Answer on page 141.

20. This player scored a game-high 31 points in the 2007 All-Star Game, the only one held to date in Las Vegas. Who was the player?

A. LeBron James

B. Kobe Bryant

C. Carmelo Anthony

D. Amar'e Stoudemire

Answer on page 141.

21. The 1973 All-Star Game in Chicago featured two future politicians. Who were they?

Answer on page 141.

22. The 1980 All-Star Game in Landover, Maryland, featured two West reserve guards who were traded for each other, straight up, after the season. Who were they?

Answer on page 141.

23. Seattle SuperSonics forward Tom Chambers erupted for a game-high 34 points to lead the West in scoring in the 1987 All-Star Game in Seattle. Which member of the Dallas Mavericks came off the bench to finish second?

Answer on page 141.

24. Who received the most votes for the 1975 NBA All-Star Game, when starters were determined by fan voting for the first time?

A. Nate Archibald

B. Bob McAdoo

C. Earl Monroe

D. Austin Carr

Answer on page 141.

25. True or False. Patrick Ewing is the last first-round pick drafted by the New York Knicks to have played in an All-Star Game.

Answer on page 141.

26. Who is the only NBA player to win an NBA Finals MVP award but never be named an NBA All-Star?
Answer on page 141.

27. Which player holds the All-Star Game single-game record for assists?
A. John Stockton
B. Chris Paul
C. Isiah Thomas
D. Magic Johnson
Answer on page 141.

28. Which player was the most recent to foul out of an All-Star Game?
A. Karl Malone
B. Russell Westbrook
C. Hakeem Olajuwon
D. Shawn Kemp
Answer on page 142.

29. Who was the leading scorer in the final Legends Game played at All-Star Weekend in 1993?
A. Otis Birdsong
B. Connie Hawkins
C. George Gervin
D. Calvin Murphy
Answer on page 142.

30. Which future NBA referee was a participant in the first Three-Point Contest at All-Star Weekend in 1986?
Answer on page 142.

31. Which player prevailed in the first Skills Challenge, which debuted during the 2003 All-Star Weekend?
A. Stephon Marbury
B. Jason Kidd

C. Gary Payton
D. Tony Parker
Answer on page 142.

32. Who was the MVP of the first ABA All-Star Game, held in 1968 at storied Hinkle Field House in Indianapolis?
A. Mel Daniels
B. Doug Moe
C. Levern Tart
D. Larry Brown
Answer on page 142.

33. In the final ABA All-Star Game in 1976, the contest featured the Denver Nuggets taking on a collection of All-Stars. Who was the Most Valuable Player?
A. Julius Erving
B. David Thompson
C. Dan Issel
D. Artis Gilmore
Answer on page 142.

34. Which player holds the NBA All-Star Game record by committing 12 turnovers?
A. Magic Johnson
B. James Harden
C. Michael Jordan
D. John Stockton
Answer on page 142.

35. Who is the only 7-foot player to win the Three-Point Contest during All-Star Weekend?
Answer on page 142.

ALL-STARS

ANSWERS

1. The first NBA All-Star Game was played in 1951 at the Boston Garden, with Ed Macauley of the Celtics earning MVP honors.

2. Kobe Bryant, with 15.

3. In the 1993 All-Star Game, John Stockton and Karl Malone of the Utah Jazz tied for game MVP.

4. While Kobe appeared in an impressive 18 All-Star Games, he is one behind the leader Kareem Abdul-Jabbar, who in his 20 seasons was a 19-time All-Star. The one year he didn't make it? That was 1978–79, when he missed the first 20 games of the season after breaking his hand in a fight with Kent Benson (a punch which broke Benson's jaw). (B)

5. During the inaugural Three-Point Contest of the 1986 All-Star Game, Larry Legend took the crown as the first to win this event. The story goes that Bird was glaring at all the other competitors before the event started, and when someone asked him why he was doing so, he replied, "I'm just trying to figure out who is going to finish in second place."

6. The easier answer was Larry Bird, who won the first three contests (1986–88). But do you know the second? Well, after Dale Ellis of the Seattle SuperSonics won it in 1989, Craig Hodges of the Chicago Bulls won it in three straight years, from 1990 to 1992.

7. Beginning in 1984, the first winner of the Slam Dunk Contest was Larry Nance of the Phoenix Suns.

8. Does one of these names stand out among the others? Well it should. While three of these stars were known for their high-flying dunks, only Nate Robinson, a 5-foot-9 guard, has won the Slam Dunk Contest three times (2006, 2009–10). (C)

9. The Miami Heat. During the 1995 All-Star Weekend, Heat shooting guard Glen Rice won the shootout, while guard Harold "Baby Jordan" Miner won his second dunk competition in three seasons.

10. I know this is a tough one. The answer is Alvan Adams, who played for the Phoenix Suns from 1975 to 1988. During his 13-year career, Adams averaged 14.1 points, 7.0 rebounds, and 4.1 assists, though his only All-Star bid was during his rookie season of 1975–76, when he averaged 19.0 points, 9.1 rebounds, 5.6 assists, 1.5 steals, and 1.5 blocks.

11. LeBron James has taken a total of 283 shots in All-Star Games. (B)

12. Elgin Baylor made 78 free throws in All-Star Games, eight more than runner-up Oscar Robertson (70). (A)

13. Moses Malone collected 44 offensive rebounds during his 13 All-Star Game appearances. (D)

14. Bob Pettit collected 178 boards in All-Star play, almost 30 more than Kareem Abdul-Jabbar, who holds the third spot among leaders. (A)

15. Magic Johnson, who passed for 127 assists in his numerous All-Star Game appearances. Chis Paul was second at 106 at the end of 2019. (B)

16. Bryant stole 38 passes in All-Star appearances, edging Jordan by one.

17. The Greek Freak, Giannis Antetokounmpo, has averaged 28.0 points per game in his first three All-Star appearances (2016–19). (A)

18. Archie Clark, who went 11 of 11 on free throws in his two All-Star Games combined (1968 and 1972). (B)

19. Rick Barry, who averaged 3.2 steals per game in All-Star play. Two other '70s stars, Walt Frazier and George McGinnis, are tied for second at 3.0.

20. Kobe Bryant outscored Amar'e Stoudemire (29), LeBron James (28), and Carmelo Anthony (20). (B)

21. Knicks forward Bill Bradley, who scored four points for the East and served three terms (1979–97) as New Jersey senator; and Pistons guard Dave Bing, who scored two for the West and later became the mayor of Detroit.

22. Paul Westphal of the Phoenix Suns and Dennis Johnson of the Seattle SuperSonics were traded for each other on June 4, 1980.

23. Rolando Blackmon, who scored 29 points.

24. Bob McAdoo of the Buffalo Braves received 98,725 fan votes, more than 11,000 ahead of runner-up John Havlicek. The game was held in Phoenix, and McAdoo scored just 11 points and committed four fouls—but at least he tied Kareem Abdul-Jabbar with a game-high 22 points the following season. (B)

25. False. David Lee, selected in the first round in 2005, appeared in the 2010 All-Star Game—his final season with the Knicks.

26. Cedric "Cornbread" Maxwell of the 1980–81 Boston Celtics.

27. During the 1984 All-Star Game, Magic Johnson recorded 22 assists, which are the most by any player. He also holds the No. 2 and No. 4 spots as well (19 in 1988 and 16 in 1983). (D)

28. During the 1987 All-Star Game, Hall of Fame center Hakeem Olajuwon fouled out with 10 points and 13 rebounds in 26 minutes of play. (C)

29. The Ice Man, George Gervin, scored 14 points in the final Legends Game played during All-Star Weekend, leading the East to a 58–45 victory. (C)

30. Leon Wood, who played six seasons in the league and remains an active official.

31. Jason Kidd, then with the New Jersey Nets, was the first winner of the All-Star Weekend Skills Challenge, finishing the course in 35.1 second. The current record is held by Deron Williams, who completed the course in 25.5 seconds. (B)

32. The MVP of the first ABA All-Star Game was Larry Brown, who finished with 17 points (as did teammate Doug Moe), three rebounds, and five assists. Even with such a great game, his West team lost to the East, 126–120. (D)

33. Leading the Nuggets to a 144–138 win, David Thompson finished with a game-high 29 points, in addition to eight rebounds and two assists, winning the MVP Award in the ABA's final All-Star Game. (B)

34. On November 19, 1990, John Stockton committed 10 turnovers in a loss to the Milwaukee Bucks. In the 1,504 regular-season games he played during his career, it was the only time he ever had 10 turnovers. *However*, Stockton committed 12 turnovers during the 1989 All-Star Game. (D)

35. During the 2006 All-Star Weekend, Dirk Nowitzki became the first (and to this day only) 7-footer to win the Three-Point Contest.

POSTSEASON

QUESTIONS

The playoffs are where champions are made. It's where players can enter the Greatest Ever conversation. It's where boys (or specifically, rookies) can become men.

Mostly, the playoffs are where the league's greatest dramas are staged—the stunning upsets, the remarkable individual performances, a place for owners and general managers to find out what needs to be done in the offseason, and finally, the pinnacle of it all for the team still standing at the end.

In the NBA, the postseason is everything.

What follows are questions and answers about the players, coaches, and teams who were at their best when it meant the most.

1. What team did the Milwaukee Bucks beat to win their only NBA championship in 1971?
   A. Knicks
   B. Bullets
   C. Celtics
   D. 76ers
   Answer on page 153.

2. Who is the only player on a losing team to win the NBA Finals MVP Award?
   Answer on page 153.

3. Which NBA player has won the most championships that was *not* a teammate of Bill Russell?
   A. Michael Jordan
   B. Robert Parish
   C. Robert Horry
   D. Kareem Abdul-Jabbar
   Answer on page 153.

4. Who were the first two African Americans to play in an NBA playoff game?
   Answer on page 153.

5. Which was the first team to win the WNBA Finals?
   A. New York Liberty
   B. Los Angeles Sparks
   C. Houston Comets
   D. Phoenix Mercury
   Answer on page 153.

6. Which player has scored the most points in a single postseason?
   A. Michael Jordan
   B. LeBron James
   C. Hakeem Olajuwon
   D. Allen Iverson
   Answer on page 154.

7. Which player has collected the most rebounds in a single postseason (since the stat was kept)?
   A. Wilt Chamberlain
   B. Bill Russell
   C. Tim Duncan
   D. Shaquille O'Neal
   Answer on page 154.

8. Which player has collected the most assists in a single postseason?
A. John Stockton
B. Rajon Rondo
C. Magic Johnson
D. LeBron James
Answer on page 154.

9. In the 1978 Finals, a player shot 0-for-14 in a Game Seven loss, then came back to win Finals MVP and lead his team to the championship in 1979. Who was it?
Answer on page 154.

10. Who is the only coach to have won championships in his first two seasons at the helm?
Answer on page 154.

11. Since the league began in 1997, there have been eight different teams to win the WNBA Finals? Do you know which teams?
Answer on page 154.

12. Of those eight teams above, two have won it four times. Which teams?
Answer on page 154.

13. In the shot-clock era (starting in 1954–55), which NBA team has scored the fewest points in a Finals game, which also paved the way for the biggest blowout in Finals history?
Answer on page 154.

14. What was the lowest seed in the playoffs to appear in the NBA Finals?
Answer on page 155.

15. What was the lowest seed in the playoffs to win the NBA Finals?
Answer on page 155.

16. Who is the only NBA player to record 40 or more rebounds in two NBA Finals games?
A. Wilt Chamberlain
B. Kevin Love
C. Moses Malone
D. Bill Russell
Answer on page 155.

17. Which team averaged just 85.3 points in the 2013 playoffs?
A. New York Knicks
B. Los Angeles Clippers
C. Indiana Pacers
D. Los Angeles Lakers
Answer on page 155.

18. Which NBA player set a league playoff record with 39 free throw attempts?
A. Patrick Ewing
B. James Harden
C. Shaquille O'Neal
D. Wes Unseld
Answer on page 155.

19. Name the first player to score at least 60 points in an NBA playoff game?
Answer on page 155.

20. Who set the playoff single-game record for the most free throws made?
A. Bob Cousy
B. Michael Jordan
C. Rick Barry
D. Chris Mullin
Answer on page 155.

21. Who holds the NBA record for games played in the playoffs with 259?
Answer on page 156.

22. Who is the only player in NBA history to score 50 or more points in back-to-back playoff games?
Answer on page 156.

23. Which player holds the NBA playoff record for highest free throw percentage?
Answer on page 156.

24. Who is the youngest player to appear in an NBA playoff game?
Answer on page 156.

25. Which NBA player holds the single-game playoff record for most minutes played?
Answer on page 156.

26. Which NBA team is the only one in league history to miss the playoffs with a winning record one season, then win the NBA title the following season?
Answer on page 156.

27. Which NBA team set a playoff record for most points in a single half?
Answer on page 156.

28. Who holds the NBA single-game record for most points scored in a playoff game?
Answer on page 156.

29. Bill Russell won a league-record 11 NBA championships, all with the Boston Celtics. Which player is next in line with 10 titles?
Answer on page 156.

30. Who threw the inbounds pass for the Philadelphia 76ers that John Havlicek of the Boston Celtics stole to seal Game Seven of the 1965 Eastern Conference finals?
Answer on page 157.

31. When the league was still known as the BAA, prior to merging with the NBL, which team won the first championship?
Answer on page 157.

32. Who has the most Finals MVPs?
A. Michael Jordan
B. Bill Russell
C. Wilt Chamberlain
D. Jerry West
Answer on page 157.

33. Which was the first team to sweep an NBA Finals series?
A. Detroit Pistons
B. Philadelphia 76ers
C. Milwaukee Bucks
D. Boston Celtics
Answer on page 157.

34. Which team has been swept the most in the NBA Finals?
A. Cleveland Cavaliers
B. Los Angeles Lakers
C. Washington Bullets
D. St. Louis Hawks
Answer on page 157.

35. What year did the Seattle SuperSonics win their lone championship?
Answer on page 157.

36. Which team beat the Boston Celtics, at the Boston Garden, in the seventh game of the Eastern Conference finals, on their way to winning the 1973 championship?
Answer on page 157. ·

37. Which team beat the Boston Celtics, at the Boston Garden, in the seventh game of the Eastern Conference finals in 1982, on their way to way to the Finals?
Answer on page 157.

38. Which team beat the Boston Celtics, at the Boston Garden, in the seventh game of the Eastern Conference finals in 2018, on their way to way to the Finals?
Answer on page 157.

39. Who was the first player to win the NBA Finals MVP Award?
Answer on page 158.

40. Who holds the NBA playoff record for most free throws made in a single game?
Answer on page 158.

41. While Boston holds the record for most NBA championships won with 17, which team has *lost* the most times in the Finals?
A. Cleveland Cavaliers
B. Washington Bullets
C. New Jersey Nets
D. Los Angeles Lakers
Answer on page 158.

42. Which player holds the record for most points scored in an NBA playoff game by a rookie?
Answer on page 158.

43. For whom is the NBA championship trophy named?
Answer on page 158.

44. Who is the youngest player to win an NBA title?
Answer on page 158.

45. Who is the oldest player to win an NBA title?
Answer on page 158.

46. Which NBA player scored 20 or more points in every Finals game in which he played?
A. Michael Jordan
B. LeBron James
C. Kobe Bryant
D. Larry Bird
Answer on page 158.

47. Who is the only player to dish 300+ assists in a single postseason?
Answer on page 158.

48. What was the first NBA Finals to go to seven games?
Answer on page 158.

49. Which team was the first to lose three consecutive NBA Finals?
Answer on page 159.

50. What is the highest win total for a team that did *not* win the NBA Finals?
Answer on page 159.

51. Which team has made the most playoff appearances?
Answer on page 159.

52. Who threw the inbounds pass to Michael Jordan for the Chicago Bulls that led to "The Shot" over Craig Ehlo of the Cleveland Cavaliers in a decisive Game Five of a 1989 playoff series at the Richfield Coliseum?
Answer on page 159.

Postseason: Questions

53. The Celtics and Lakers have won the most NBA titles with 17 and 16, respectively. Which team sits in third for most championships won?
Answer on page 159.

54. Which team has the lowest winning percentage to go on and win the NBA Finals?
Answer on page 159.

151

POSTSEASON

ANSWERS

1. The Bucks only championship was in 1971, when they swept the Baltimore Bullets. (B)

2. Jerry West's Los Angeles Lakers lost to the Boston Celtics in seven games in the 1969 NBA Finals. West averaged 37.9 PPG for the series, earning him Finals MVP.

3. Bill Russell won an incredible 11 championships during his 13-year career. In fact, aside from Russell, only eight players have won 7+ championships in their careers, and *all but one* were teammates of the great Russell. So who is that one player? What great was able to accomplish such a feat? Well, they didn't call him "Big Shot Bob" for nothing. Yes, Robert Horry collected seven championships during his 16-year career. In fact, he made the playoffs in every season of his career, and his teams never were eliminated in the first round. (C)

4. Jim Tucker and Earl Lloyd were the first two African Americans to appear in an NBA playoff game, doing so with the Syracuse Nationals in 1955.

5. The Houston Comets took down the Charlotte Sting in the semis and defeated the New York Liberty in the finals to become the league's first champions. (C)

6. In the 1991–92 NBA playoffs, Michael Jordan scored a total of 759 points, averaging 34.5 per playoff game. (A)

7. In the 1968–69 NBA playoffs, Wilt Chamberlain collected a total of 444 rebounds, averaging 19.2 per playoff game. (A)

8. In the 1987–88 NBA playoffs, Magic Johnson collected a total of 303 assists, averaging 12.6 per playoff game. (C)

9. In Game Seven of the 1978 NBA Finals, Dennis Johnson shot 0-for-14 from the floor as his Seattle SuperSonics lost to the Washington Bullets. The following season, his Sonics had their revenge, as they beat the Bullets in five games in the 1979 Finals. Johnson averaged 22.6 points, 6.0 rebounds, 6.0 assists, 1.8 steals, and 2.2 blocks for the series, taking home Finals MVP.

10. Coach John Kundla won championships in his first two seasons as head coach of the Minneapolis Lakers, in 1948–49 and 1949–50. While the Lakers did not win the following season, they responded with three straight after that (1951–52, 1952–53, and 1953–54).

11 and 12. In the 22 years of the WNBA, there have been eight different champions. But which two have won it four times? Below is the breakdown:

Houston Comets* (1997, 1998, 1999, 2000)
Los Angeles Sparks (2001, 2002, 2016)
Detroit Shock (2003, 2006, 2008)
Seattle Storm (2004, 2010, 2018)
Sacramento Monarchs (2005)
Phoenix Mercury (2007, 2009, 2014)
Minnesota Lynx* (2011, 2013, 2015, 2017)
Indiana Fever (2012)

13. On June 7, 1998, the Chicago Bulls defeated the Utah Jazz in Game Three of the NBA Finals, 96–54. The Bulls would go on to win the series in six games, winning their third consecutive championship.

14. In a lockout-shortened season, the 1998–99 New York Knicks went 27–23, which gave them the No. 8 seed by a single game over the Charlotte Hornets. In the first round, they defeated the No. 1 seeded Miami Heat in five games; in the conference semifinals they defeated the No. 4 seeded Atlanta Hawks in four games; in the conference finals they defeated the No. 2 seeded Indiana Pacers in six games. Unfortunately for them, after such a stellar run, they ran into the No. 1 seeded San Antonio Spurs, who defeated them in five games.

15. The 1994–95 Houston Rockets were ranked the No. 6 seed going into the playoffs. In the first round they defeated the No. 3 seeded Utah Jazz in five games; in the conference semifinals they defeated the No. 2 seeded Phoenix Suns in seven games; in the conference finals they defeated the No. 1 seeded San Antonio Spurs; and in the NBA Finals they defeated the Orlando Magic in four games, who were the No. 1 seed from the East.

16. Bill Russell of the Boston Celtics, who did so against the St. Louis Hawks in 1960 and the Los Angeles Lakers in 1962. (D)

17. During a season in which the team had three different coaches, the No. 7 seed Los Angeles Lakers scored 79, 91, 89, and 82 points against the No. 2 San Antonio Spurs, getting swept in the first round. (D)

18. That would be Shaquille O'Neal, as a member of the Los Angeles Lakers, when the Indiana Pacers went to the "Hack a Shaq" on June 9, 2000. O'Neal shot 18 of 39 from the line that night. (C)

19. Elgin Baylor of the Los Angeles Lakers scored 61 points on April 14, 1962, against the Boston Celtics in Game Five of the NBA Finals.

20. Bob Cousy of the Boston Celtics, who made 30 free throws against the Syracuse Nationals on on March 21, 1953, in a four-overtime play-off foul-fest. (A)

21. With five rings (as a member of the Lakers), Derek Fisher holds the current record for games played in the playoffs. During his 18-year career, his teams only missed the playoffs twice.

22. Michael Jordan of the Chicago Bulls scored 50 and 55 points, respectively, in Games One and Two of the 1988 first-round series against the Cleveland Cavaliers.

23. Mark Price of the Cleveland Cavaliers, with a 94.39 playoff free-throw percentage. His regular-season average was 90.4 percent.

24. That would be Andrew Bynum of the Los Angeles Lakers, who was 18 years and 191 days old when his team faced the Phoenix Suns on May 6, 2006.

25. Kevin Johnson of the Phoenix Suns played 62 minutes on June 13, 1993, in a triple-overtime game against the Chicago Bulls.

26. The Golden State Warriors are the only team to miss the playoffs with a winning record one year and then win the NBA title the following season. They won the title in 1975 after missing the 1974 playoffs with a 44–38 record (.537 winning percentage) the previous year.

27. The Cleveland Cavaliers scored 86 points in the first half of Game Four of the NBA Finals against the Golden State Warriors on June 9, 2017.

28. Michael Jordan was at it again when he scored 63 points against the Boston Celtics in a first-round game on April 20, 1986, at the Boston Garden. However, his Bulls lost, 135–131.

29. Sam Jones has 10 rings, and won them as . . . you guessed it . . . a teammate of Bill Russell. In fact, the seven players who have the most rings after Russell were all Celtics teammates.

30. Hal Greer made the errant pass that helped the Celtics move on in the 1965 playoffs.

31. The Philadelphia Warriors were the first to take the crown for the 1946–47 season, defeating the Chicago Stags in five games.

32. Michael Jordan was named Finals MVP six times (1991–93, 1996–98). (A)

33. While each of those franchises has swept a Finals series, the Boston Celtics were the first—a feat they accomplished in 1958–59 against the Minneapolis Lakers. (D)

34. The Los Angeles Lakers have been swept three times—the first as the Minneapolis Lakers in 1958–59 (by the Boston Celtics). They were swept twice in the Finals after moving to Los Angeles (1982–83 by the Philadelphia 76ers and 1988–89 by the Detroit Pistons). The Cleveland Cavaliers and Washington Bullets, by the way, have each been swept twice (Cavs by the Spurs and Warriors, and Bullets by the Bucks and Warriors). (B)

35. The Sonics, coached by Hall of Famer Lenny Wilkens, won their lone title in 1979, avenging a defeat by the Washington Bullets in the previous year's championship series.

36. The New York Knicks took down the Celtics in the seventh game of the Eastern Conference finals, then defeated the Los Angeles Lakers in five games.

37. The Philadelphia 76ers took down the Celtics in the seventh game of the Eastern Conference finals, yet lost to the Los Angeles Lakers in six games.

38. The Cleveland Cavaliers took down the Celtics in the seventh game of the Eastern Conference finals, yet lost to the Golden State Warriors in four games.

39. Jerry West of the Los Angeles Lakers in 1968–69.

40. Bob Cousy of the Boston Celtics, who made 30 shots from the line against the Syracuse Nationals in a quadruple-overtime game March 21, 1953. Cousy made 30 of 32 on free throws, helping lift Boston to a 111–105 victory.

41. The Los Angeles Lakers, with 15. (D)

42. Wilt Chamberlain of the Philadelphia Warriors, who poured in 53 points against the Syracuse Nationals on March 14, 1960.

43. The trophy was originally named the NBA Finals Trophy, then changed to the Walter A. Brown Trophy in 1964, and renamed again in 1984 in honor of former commissioner Larry O'Brien, who served from 1975 through 1983.

44. Darko Miličić of the 2003–04 Detroit Pistons, at 18 years and 361 days old. Of course, Miličić is mostly known for being the No. 2 overall pick behind LeBron James (and ahead of Carmelo Anthony, Chris Bosh, and Dwyane Wade) in the 2003 draft.

45. Robert Parish of the Chicago Bulls in 1996–97, at 43 years old.

46. Michael Jordan, who played in 35 Finals games and scored at least 20 each time. (A)

47. Averaging 12.4 assists over 24 playoff games, Magic Johnson is the only player to record more than 300 assists (304) in a single postseason, accomplishing this feat for the 1987–88 Lakers. His highs were 20, 19 (twice), and 18, while only missing double digits five times (two games with nine and three with six).

48. In 1950–51, when the Rochester Royals defeated the New York Knicks, 4–3.

49. The New York Knicks in 1950–51, 1951–52, and 1952–53.

50. With 73 wins, breaking the record of the 1995–96 Chicago Bulls (who went 72–10), the 2015–16 Golden State Warriors have the most wins of any team in NBA history. However, they lost in the Finals in seven games to LeBron James and the Cleveland Cavaliers.

51. The Minneapolis/Los Angeles Lakers, with 58.

52. Brad Sellers, who grew up in Warrensville Heights, just 17 miles outside of Cleveland, and played his college ball at Ohio State.

53. The Chicago Bulls with six—all coming during the Michael Jordan era (1991, 1992, 1993, 1996, 1997, and 1998).

54. Finishing the season with a 44–38 record (.537 winning percentage), the 1977–78 Washington Bullets defeated the Seattle SuperSonics in seven games to take home the title.

FOURTH QUARTER

AWARD WINNERS

QUESTIONS

In sports, Most Valuable Player of an entire league is the highest honor that exists. But in the NBA, there are many other ways to show what you have achieved in a particular season.

Along with MVP, the league hands out the following awards annually:

- Rookie of the Year
- Defensive Player of the Year
- Sixth Man of the Year
- Most Improved Player
- All-Star Game MVP
- Finals MVP
- Teammate of the Year
- Citizenship Award

Those are just for the players. The league also hands out Coach of the Year and Executive of the Year awards at the end of each season. With the exception of Teammate of the Year and Executive of the Year, all of the awards are voted on by sportswriters/media members who cover the NBA. (The Teammate and Executive Awards are selected by the player's and executive's peers.)

In the NBA, when you don't win a championship, an individual accolade is the next best thing. See how much you know about the league's all-time individual awards in the pages that follow.

1. Which player has won the most MVP Awards?
   A. Michael Jordan
   B. Wilt Chamberlain
   C. Kareem Abdul-Jabbar
   D. Bill Russell
   Answer on page 173.

2. Who are the only three players to win three consecutive MVP Awards?
   Answer on page 173.

3. Which MVP had the lowest points per game average?
   Answer on page 173.

4. Which MVP had the highest steals per game average?
   Answer on page 173.

5. There have been seven times when the league MVP averaged more than 10 assists a game. But who was the youngest? Who was the oldest?
   Answer on page 173.

6. There have been 28 players who have won Rookie of the Year honors and later ended up in the HOF. How many can you name?
   Answer on page 174.

7. Which team has had the most league MVPs?
   A. Boston Celtics
   B. New York Knicks
   C. Chicago Bulls
   D. Los Angeles Lakers
   Answer on page 174.

8. Three women have won the WNBA MVP Award three times. Who are they?
   Answer on page 174.

9. Which player has won the Sixth Man of the Year Award the most?
   A. Kevin McHale
   B. Detlef Schrempf
   C. Jamal Crawford
   D. Manu Ginóbili
   Answer on page 175.

10. Who was the first player to leave their team after an MVP season?
    Answer on page 175.

11. Only three player have ever won the MVP Award with more than one team. Who are they?
    Answer on page 175.

12. Who are the only two players to win both the Sixth Man Award and MVP in their careers?
    Answer on page 175.

13. Who are the only three players to win the Sixth Man Award that are in the HOF?
    Answer on page 175.

14. Who was the only player with multiple assist titles in the 1970s?
    Answer on page 175.

15. Which player had the most rebound titles in the 1970s?
    Answer on page 175.

16. Which player has the longest consecutive scoring-title streak?
    Answer on page 175.

17. This three-time league MVP earned the honor in back-to-back seasons playing for different teams. Who was he?
    Answer on page 175.

18. For whom is the NBA's Coach of the Year Award named?
    Answer on page 175.

19. Wilt Chamberlain was named NBA Most Valuable Player and Rookie of the Year in the same season, 1959–60. Who was the next player to gain such an honor?
    A. Elvin Hayes
    B. Wes Unseld
    C. Bob McAdoo
    D. LeBron James
    Answer on page 175.

20. Which player was the first to win league MVP by a unanimous vote?
    A. Stephen Curry
    B. Michael Jordan
    C. Wilt Chamberlain
    D. LeBron James
    Answer on page 176.

21. Who was the only member of the Harlem Globetrotters to win league MVP?
    A. Curly Neal
    B. Meadowlark Lemon
    C. Earl Mornroe
    D. Wilt Chamberlain
    Answer on page 176.

22. When did Larry Bird win his first of three straight MVP Awards?
    Answer on page 176.

23. Charlie Scott was ABA co-Rookie of the Year in 1970–71. Who was the future NBA head coach who shared the award with Scott?
    Answer on page 176.

24. Who was the first WNBA ROY to win an MVP Award?
A. Maya Moore
B. Candace Parker
C. Tamika Catchings
D. Chamique Holdsclaw
Answer on page 176.

25. Who won the NBA's first Most Improved Player Award in 1986?
Answer on page 176.

26. Who was the first foreign-born player to win the Most Improved Player Award?
Answer on page 176.

27. Which team had three players win the Most Improved Player Award between 2009 and 2018?
Answer on page 176.

28. Who is the only member of the Milwaukee Bucks to win the NBA's Most Improved Player Award (through 2019)?
Answer on page 176–177.

29. Who is the only former No. 1 overall pick to win the Most Improved Player Award?
Answer on page 177.

30. Who won the Defensive Player of the Year Award in each of the first two seasons it existed, in 1983 and '84?
Answer on page 177.

31. Who was the first player listed as a forward to be named Defensive Player of the Year?
Answer on page 177.

32. Who was the first second-round draft pick to be named Defensive Player of the Year?
Answer on page 177.

33. Who was the first foreign-born player to be named Defensive Player of the Year?
Answer on page 177.

34. Three members of the San Antonio Spurs have won Defensive Player of the Year. Can you name them?
Answer on page 177.

35. Only one member of the Miami Heat has been named Defensive Player of the Year, but he won the award in back-to-back seasons. Who was it?
Answer on page 177.

36. Who is the only player to have won the Defensive Player of the Year Award three straight seasons, between 2008 and 2011?
Answer on page 177.

37. Who was named the NBA's Sixth Man of the Year when it was first awarded in 1983?
Answer on page 177.

38. Boston Celtics legend Kevin McHale is one of only two players to win the Sixth Man of the Year Award in back-to-back seasons (1984 and '85). The other player did it in 1991 and '92. Who is he?
Answer on page 177.

39. Who is the only member of the Memphis Grizzlies to be named Sixth Man of the Year?
Answer on page 177.

40. Three members of the New York Knicks have been named Sixth Man of the Year. Who are they?
Answer on page 178.

41. Only one member of the Houston Rockets has won Sixth Man of the Year. Who is he?
Answer on page 178.

42. Which former No. 1 overall pick was named NBA Sixth Man of the Year in 1998?
Answer on page 178.

43. Who is the only father of a modern-day player to win Sixth Man of the Year?
Answer on page 178.

44. Starting with Bob McAdoo in 1973, the Buffalo Braves had three players named Rookie of the Year in a span of five seasons. Ernie DiGregorio followed McAdoo the following season. Who is the third player?
Answer on page 178.

45. Name the only player from Kansas State who was named Rookie of the Year.
Answer on page 178.

46. Who is the only second-round pick since 2000 to be named Rookie of the Year?
Answer on page 178.

47. Who is the only Rookie of the Year in Utah Jazz history?
Answer on page 178.

48. Derrick Coleman became the second player in the history of the New Jersey Nets to win Rookie of the Year, winning the award in 1991. The first won it nine years earlier. Name him.
Answer on page 178.

49. Three straight point guards won Rookie of the Year, from 2012 to 2014. Who were they?
Answer on page 178.

50. Tyreke Evans was the only member of the Sacramento Kings ever named Rookie of the Year, winning the award in 2010. But one player won it as a member of the Kansas City Kings back in 1979. Who was it?
Answer on page 178.

51. Magic Johnson was named MVP three times in four seasons (1987, 1989, 1990). Who won the award in 1988?
Answer on page 178.

52. LeBron James won league MVP four times in five seasons (2009, 2010, 2012, 2013). Who won the award in 2011?
Answer on page 178.

53. Kareem Abdul-Jabbar was named league MVP five times between 1971 and 1977. Who were the only two other players to win the award during that stretch?
Answer on page 179.

54. Who was the only player to win his lone league MVP a season after winning his lone championship?
Answer on page 179.

55. Who is the first foreign-born player to win league MVP?
Answer on page 179.

56. True or False. Shaquille O'Neal was never named league MVP with the Orlando Magic.
Answer on page 179.

57. Which NBA player was the first to win the scoring and rebounding titles, and be named league MVP in the same season?
Answer on page 179.

58. Who is the only NBA player to win the scoring and rebounding titles, and be named MVP in the same season more than once?
Answer on page 179.

59. Who was the first NBA player to win five MVP Awards?
Answer on page 179.

60. Who are the only players to win league MVP, Finals MVP, and an Olympic Gold medal in the same year?
Answer on page 179.

61. Which league MVP has the lowest field goal percentage in the three-point era?
A. Allen Iverson
B. Russell Westbrook
C. Michael Jordan
D. Kobe Bryant
Answer on page 179.

62. Who is the oldest player to win the MVP Award?
A. Karl Malone
B. Steve Nash
C. Michael Jordan
D. Hakeem Olajuwon
Answer on page 179.

63. Who was the first NBA Rookie of the Year?
Answer on page 179.

64. Who was the first NBA player to be named All-Star Game MVP, league MVP, and Finals MVP in the same season?
Answer on page 180.

65. Who is the only player to win the the awards for Sixth Man of the Year and Most Improved Player in the same season?
Answer on page 180.

AWARD WINNERS

ANSWERS

1. While both Michael Jordan and Bill Russell have five MVPs to their name (with Wilt having four), Kareem Abdul-Jabbar leads them all with six (1970–71, 1971–72, 1973–74, 1975–76, 1976–77, 1979–80). (C)

2. While we noted above that Kareem won a total of six, the three to win back-to-back-to-back MVP Awards are Bill Russell (1960–61, 1961–62, 1962–63), Wilt Chamberlain (1965–66, 1966–67, 1967–68), and Larry Bird (1983–84, 1984–85, 1985–86).

3. Wes Unseld, 1968–69, 13.8 points per game.

4. Michael Jordan, 1987–88, 3.2 steals per game.

5. Four players have averaged more than 10 assists for a season in which they won league MVP. The youngest to do so was Oscar Robertson, who in the 1963–64 season averaged 11 assists a game. (Fun fact: Both Robertson and Derrick Rose were 22 when they won the award, but O gets the nod as he was born in March while Rose was born in October.)

   The oldest was Steve Nash, who in the 2005–06 season averaged 10.5 assists a game. The other two? Magic Johnson (who did it three times) and Russell Westbrook. (Nash also won the award while averaging more than 10 a game for the 2004–05 season.)

6.

Bob Pettit (ROY: 1954–55; HOF: 1971)
Maurice Stokes (ROY: 1955–56; HOF: 2004)
Tom Heinsohn (ROY: 1956–57; HOF: 2015)
Elgin Baylor (ROY: 1958–59; HOF: 1977)
Wilt Chamberlain (ROY: 1959–60; HOF: 1979)
Oscar Robertson (ROY: 1960–61; HOF: 1980)
Walt Bellamy (ROY: 1961–62; HOF: 1993)
Jerry Lucas (ROY: 1963–64; HOF: 1980)
Rick Barry (ROY: 1965–66; HOF: 1987)
Dave Bing (ROY: 1966–67; HOF: 1990)
Earl Monroe (ROY: 1967–68; HOF: 1990)
Wes Unseld (ROY: 1968–69; HOF: 1988)
Kareem Abdul-Jabbar (ROY: 1969–70; HOF: 1995)
Dave Cowens (ROY: 1970–71; HOF: 1991)
Bob McAdoo (ROY: 1972–73; HOF: 2000)
Jamaal Wilkes (ROY: 1974–75; HOF: 2012)
Adrian Dantley (ROY: 1976–77; HOF: 2008)
Larry Bird (ROY: 1979–80; HOF: 1998)
Ralph Sampson (ROY: 1983–84; HOF: 2012)
Michael Jordan (ROY: 1984–85; HOF: 2009)
Patrick Ewing (ROY: 1985–86; HOF: 2008)
Mitch Richmond (ROY: 1988–89; HOF: 2014)
David Robinson (ROY: 1989–90; HOF: 2009)
Shaquille O'Neal (ROY: 1992–93; HOF: 2016)
Grant Hill (ROY: 1994–95; HOF: 2018)
Jason Kidd (ROY: 1994–95; HOF: 2018)
Allen Iverson (ROY: 1996–97; HOF: 2016)

7. While the Lakers have had eight MVPs and the Bulls six, the Boston Celtics lead the way with 10 MVPs. Surprisingly, the Knicks have only had one, which was Willis Reed for the 1969–70 season. (A)

8. Sheryl Swoopes (2000, 2002, 2005), Lisa Leslie (2001, 2004, 2006), and Lauren Jackson (2003, 2007, 2010).

9. Jamal Crawford is the only player to have won the Sixth Man of the Year Award three times (2009–10, 2013–14, 2015–16). (C)

10. After winning the MVP Award—his fourth—for the 1967–68 season as a member of the Philadelphia 76ers, Wilt Chamberlain took his talents to the West Coast, joining the Los Angeles Lakers.

11. Kareem Abdul-Jabbar (Bucks: 1970–71, 1971–72, 1973–74; Lakers: 1975–76 1976–77, 1979–80), LeBron James (Cavaliers: 2008–09, 2009–10; Heat: 2011–12, 2012–13), and Moses Malone (Rockets: 1978–79, 1981–82; 76ers: 1982–83).

12. Bill Walton was named MVP for the 1977–78 season, and the sixth-man for the 1985–86 season; James Harden was named MVP for the 2017–18 season, and the sixth-man for the 2011–12 season.

13. While Manu Ginóbili will get there, Bill Walton, Kevin McHale, and Bobby Jones are the only three men to win the Sixth Man Award and be inducted into the HOF.

14. That would be Kevin Porter, who did so in 1974–75, 1977–78, and 1978–79.

15. That would be Wilt Chamberlain, who did so in 1970–71, 1971–72, and 1972–73.

16. Wilt Chamberlain, who led the league in scoring in the first seven seasons of his career, starting in his rookie campaign of 1959–60.

17. Moses Malone, who won the MVP in 1981–82 with the Houston Rockets and in 1982–83 with the Philadelphia 76ers. He also won the award in 1978–79 as a member of the Rockets.

18. After leading the Boston Celtics as both a coach and executive for several decades, which included double-digit championships, the NBA named its Coach of the Year Award after Red Auerbach.

19. Wes Unseld, who accomplish this feat with the Baltimore Bullets during the 1968–69 season. (B)

20. Stephen Curry won the league MVP by a unanimous vote in 2016 after leading the Golden State Warriors to a record-setting 73–9 season. Curry and the Warriors did not win the title that season, however, losing in the Finals to the Cleveland Cavaliers in seven games. (A)

21. Wilt Chamberlain played with the Harlem Globetrotters for one season (1958–59) before joining the NBA and winning four league MVP Awards. (D)

22. Bird won his first MVP for the 1983–84 season, when the Boston Celtics legend averaged 28.7 points, 10.5 rebounds, and 6.6 assists on the way to a championship.

23. Dan Issel of the Kentucky Colonels, who went on to play for and coach the Denver Nuggets.

24. Not only did Candace Parker become the first ROY to also win the MVP Award, but she did it in the *same season!* In 2008, Parker averaged 18.5 points, 9.5 rebounds, 3.4 assists, 2.3 blocks, and 1.3 steals in an incredible rookie campaign that saw her also hoist the MVP trophy. (B)

25. Alvin Robertson of the San Antonio Spurs, who essentially doubled is statistical output from his rookie season of 1984–85.

26. Gheorghe Mureşan of the Washington Bullets in 1996, who increased his points (10.0 to 14.5) and rebounds (6.7 to 9.6) from the previous season.

27. The Indiana Pacers, with Danny Granger (2009), Paul George (2013), and Victor Oladipo (2018) winning the award. They've had a league-high five players win it overall, with Jalen Rose (2000) and Jermaine O'Neal (2002) also winning the award as members of the Pacers.

28. After increasing his points (16.9 to 22.9), rebounds (7.7 to 8.8), assists (4.3 to 5.4), field goal percentage (.506 to .521), and receiving his first All-Star nod, Giannis Antetokounmpo won the Most Improved Player Award in 2017.

29. Pervis Ellison of the Washington Bullets in 1992. Ellison was originally drafted by the Sacramento Kings with the top overall pick in 1986.

30. Sidney Moncrief of the Milwaukee Bucks.

31. Michael Cooper of the Los Angeles Lakers, who won the award in 1987.

32. Dennis Rodman of the Detroit Pistons in 1989. He also won it the following season.

33. Dikembe Mutombo of the Atlanta Hawks in 1995. Mutombo won the award three times during his 18-year career.

34. Alvin Robertson (1986), David Robinson (1992), and Kawhi Leonard (2015 and 2016).

35. Alonzo Mourning, who won the award in 1997 and '98.

36. That would be eight-time All-Star Dwight Howard, who won his three-consecutive DPOY awards with the Orlando Magic.

37. With no starts in 74 games, Bobby Jones averaged 9.0 points, 4.6 rebounds, and 1.9 assists in 23.6 minutes off the bench with the Philadelphia 76ers.

38. German-born Detlef Schrempf accomplished this feat as a member of the Indiana Pacers.

39. Averaging 13.7 pounds, 5.4 rebounds, and 2.7 assists in 30.6 minutes per game, Mike Miller won the award for the 2005–06 season, still the only Grizzlies player to do so.

40. Anthony Mason (1995), John Starks (1997), and J. R. Smith (2013).

41. Averaging 16.2 points, 2.7 rebounds, and 2.5 assists in 31.0 minutes per game, Eric Gordon of the Houston Rockets won the award for the 2016–17 season.

42. Danny Manning of the Phoenix Suns. Manning was drafted by the Clippers with the top pick in 1989.

43. Dell Curry of the Charlotte Hornets in 1994. Curry is the father of Golden State Warriors guard Stephen Curry and Dallas Mavericks guard Seth Curry.

44. Adrian Dantley, who was named Rookie of the Year in 1977.

45. Mitch Richmond of the Golden State Warriors in 1989.

46. Malcolm Brogdon of the Milwaukee Bucks in 2016, who was drafted with the No. 36 overall pick.

47. Darrell Griffith, who won the award in 1980 after averaging 20.6 points for the season coming off the bench.

48. Third overall pick Buck Williams won the award in 1982, averaging 15.5 points and 12.3 rebounds while starting all 82 games.

49. Kyrie Irving of the Cleveland Cavaliers (2012), Damian Lillard of the Portland Trail Blazers (2013), and Michael Carter-Williams of the Philadelphia 76ers (2014).

50. Phil Ford.

51. The award-winner is a different MJ. That would be Michael Jordan, who won the 1988 MVP Award with the Chicago Bulls.

52. Derrick Rose of the Chicago Bulls.

53. Dave Cowens of the Boston Celtics (1973) and Bob McAdoo of the Buffalo Braves (1975).

54. Bill Walton of the Portland Trail Blazers, who won the award in 1978.

55. Nigerian-born Hakeem Olajuwon was the first foreign-born player to win league MVP as a member of the Houston Rockets in 1994.

56. True. O'Neal won the award just once—in 2000, as a member of the Los Angeles Lakers.

57. Bob Pettit of the St. Louis Hawks, who averaged 25.7 points and 16.2 rebounds to win league MVP for the 1955–56 season.

58. Wilt Chamberlain, who did so with the Philadelphia Warriors in 1959–60 and again with the Philadelphia 76ers in 1965–66.

59. Bill Russell of the Boston Celtics, who won his fifth MVP Award in the 1964–65 season.

60. Michael Jordan and LeBron James.

61. The reason we specified is that the 1956–57 MVP Award went to Bob Cousy, who averaged 20.6 points, 7.5 assists, and 4.8 rebounds for the Boston Celtics—though he had a .378 field goal percentage. So, the player with the lowest since the three-point shot was brought into the league is Allen Iverson, who during his MVP season of 2000–01 shot .420 from the field.

62. At 35 years of age, Karl Malone won the MVP Award for the 1998–99 season. He also is the third-oldest to win the award (Jordan is second at 34) when he won it in 1996–97 at the age of 33. (A)

63. Don "Monk" Meineke of the Fort Wayne Pistons in 1952–53, who averaged 10.7 points, 6.9 rebounds, and 2.2 assists.

64. Willis Reed of the New York Knicks, who accomplished this trifecta for the 1969–70 season.

65. Darrell Armstrong became the first and only player to ever win the awards for Six Man of the Year and Most Improved Player in the same season, when he did so as a member of the Orlando Magic in 1998–99.

RECORDS

QUESTIONS

Once an NBA player reaches a certain level of individual greatness, has a certain degree of team success, and makes a certain number of millions, he tends to still be motivated by one thing:

Legacy.

Where does he stand on the all-time scoring chart? How about rebounds and assists? And how many championships does he own?

All of these are important questions for legends when approaching the ends of their careers. Basically, they want their accomplishments to be remembered—and the best way to do that is to put their names in the record books, to reach and set milestones.

For instance, a lot of younger fans may not have known one-time Denver Nuggets scoring machine Alex English until LeBron James approached English on the NBA's all-time scoring list. Suddenly, English's name had been making the rounds, with everyone talking about how James was about to pass him in career points.

For the record, James overtook English in that very category in December 2015. But that's just very specific example to make a larger point.

Namely, that whether you're a player, team, or coach, record setting is one underrated aspect to stay in the game.

What follows is some trivia on who set the standards, both high and low, throughout history.

1. Name the first player to score 2,000 or more points in a single season.
Answer on page 193.

2. Between the 1946–47 and 1968–69 seasons, only two players led the league in both scoring and rebounding for the same season. Who were they?
Answer on page 193.

3. There have been a total of four NBA players to record a quadruple-double. Can you name the first to accomplish this feat?
Answer on page 193.

4. Can you name the other three to do so?
Answer on page 193.

5. Who is the only player to have recorded a triple-double while playing less than 30 minutes?
Answer on page 193.

6. Aside from the player above, who are the other five players to record a triple-double while shooting 1.000 from the field?
Answer on page 194.

7. Who was the first player to score 20 or more points in 50 consecutive playoff games?
A. Michael Jordan
B. Kareem Abdul-Jabbar
C. Wilt Chamberlain
D. Karl Malone
Answer on page 194.

8. Who was the first NBA player to record at least 10 steals in a game?
A. Jerry West
B. Alvin Robertson
C. Dave Bing
D. Mo Cheeks
Answer on page 194.

9. Two players share the NBA record for most assists in a quarter with 14. Who were they?
   Answer on page 194.

10. What player holds the record for most consecutive double-doubles in one season since the NBA/ABA merger?
    Answer on page 194.

11. Which NBA player is alone in league history by fouling out in only three minutes of playing time?
    Answer on page 194.

12. Who holds the NBA record for most missed field goals in a single game?
    A. Detlef Schrempf
    B. Tim Hardaway Jr.
    C. Joe Fulks
    D. Mookie Blaylock
    Answer on page 194.

13. Which NBA player holds the record for most free throws made in a single game without a miss?
    Answer on page 194.

14. Two players occupy the top 12 slots in terms of single-game rebounds. Who were they?
    Answer on page 194.

15. Who was the only player, aside from Chamberlain and Russell, to have 40 or more rebounds in a game?
    Answer on page 194.

16. Which player holds the league record for average minutes played in postseason history?
    Answer on page 194.

17. Who is the only NBA player to score at least 20,000 points while averaging less than 15 points per game?
Answer on page 195.

18. Which player became the first to lead the NCAA, ABA, and NBA in scoring?
Answer on page 195.

19. Who is the NBA's all-time leader in personal fouls?
A. Karl Malone
B. Charles Oakley
C. Robert Parish
D. Kareem Abdul-Jabbar
Answer on page 195.

20. Who is the only player to win two championships in the dual role of player-coach?
A. Bob Cousy
B. Tom Heinsohn
C. Bill Russell
D. Lenny Wilkens
Answer on page 195.

21. True or False. At 7-foot-7, Manute Bol is the tallest NBA player of all time.
Answer on page 195.

22. Who has the highest points per game average for a single season in WNBA history?
A. Diana Taurasi
B. Maya Moore
C. Cynthia Cooper
D. Brittney Griner
Answer on page 195.

23. Who has the highest assists per game average for a single season in WNBA history?
Answer on page 195.

24. Courney Vandersloot is one of only two players to ever average 8.0 assists or more for a season. Who is the other?
Answer on page 195.

25. Who has the highest rebound average for a single season in WNBA history?
A. Sylvia Fowles
B. Jonquel Jones
C. Tina Charles
D. Chamique Holdsclaw
Answer on page 196.

26. Which player holds the record for most four-point plays?
A. Kobe Bryant
B. Reggie Miller
C. Jamal Crawford
D. J. J. Redick
Answer on page 196.

27. Who has the most points in WNBA history?
A. Cappie Pondexter
B. Tina Thompson
C. Diana Taurasi
D. Candice Dupree
Answer on page 196.

28. Who has the most assists in WNBA history?
A. Diana Taurasi
B. Sue Bird
C. Becky Hammon
D. Ticha Penicheiro
Answer on page 196.

29. Who has the most rebounds in WNBA history?
A. Lisa Leslie
B. Tina Thompson
C. Tamika Catchings
D. Rebekkah Brunson
Answer on page 196.

30. Who has the most steals in WNBA history?
A. Ticha Penicheiro
B. Sheryl Swoopes
C. Alana Beard
D. Tamika Catchings
Answer on page 196.

31. Who has the most blocks in WNBA history?
A. Lisa Leslie
B. Margo Dydek
C. Brittney Griner
D. Lauren Jackson
Answer on page 196.

32. Who was the first player in NBA history to score 2,000 points in a season?
Answer on page 196.

33. Who holds the Philadelphia 76ers career record for blocked shots?
A. Charles Barkley
B. Samuel Dalembert
C. Julius Erving
D. Theo Ratliff
Answer on page 197.

34. Who led the Miami Heat in scoring at the end of their expansion season of 1988–89?
A. Rory Sparrow
B. Kevin Edwards
C. Glen Rice
D. Pearl Washington
Answer on page 197.

35. Who is the shortest player to lead the NBA in rebounding?
Answer on page 197.

36. Who is the Denver Nuggets' all-time leading scorer?
A. Alex English
B. Carmelo Anthony
C. Dan Issel
D. David Thompson
Answer on page 197.

37. Who is the Vancouver/Memphis Grizzlies' all-time leading scorer?
A. Zach Randolph
B. Pau Gasol
C. Marc Gasol
D. Shareef Abdur-Rahim
Answer on page 197.

38. Bill Russell is the Boston Celtics' all-time leading rebounder with 21,620 for his career. Who is second?
A. Larry Bird
B. Dave Cowens
C. Robert Parish
D. Kevin McHale
Answer on page 197.

39. Before moving to Sacramento, the Kings played in Kansas City from 1972 to 1985. Can you name the player who scored the most points during that span?
    A. Larry Drew
    B. Jimmy Walker
    C. Nate Archibald
    D. Scott Wedman
    Answer on page 197.

40. Who is the youngest player to have back-to-back 50-point games?
    A. LeBron James
    B. Devin Booker
    C. Wilt Chamberlain
    D. Michael Jordan
    Answer on page 197.

41. Who is the oldest player to score 50 points in a game?
    A. Michael Jordan
    B. Larry Bird
    C. Bernard King
    D. Moses Malone
    Answer on page 197.

42. Who is the oldest player to score more than 50 points in a game?
    A. Michael Jordan
    B. Alex English
    C. Karl Malone
    D. Kobe Bryant
    Answer on page 198.

43. We all know that Wilt Chamberlain scored 100 points in a game and that Kobe Bryant scored 81, but do you know who has scored the third-most points in a game in NBA history?
    Answer on page 198.

44. Who holds the ABA's highest single-season scoring average?
   A. George McGinnis
   B. Rick Barry
   C. Charlie Scott
   D. Julius Erving
   Answer on page 198.

45. LeBron James is the Cleveland Cavaliers' all-time leading scorer with 23,119 points. Who is second?
   Answer on page 198.

46. Who is the Philadelphia 76ers' all-time franchise leading scorer?
   Answer on page 198.

47. Michael Jordan, Scottie Pippen, and Bob Love are the top three career scoring leaders, respectively, in Chicago Bulls history. Who is fourth?
   Answer on page 198.

48. Reggie Miller is the Indiana Pacers' career scoring leader with 25,279 points. Which of his former teammates is second?
   Answer on page 198.

49. Who is the only former member of the Cleveland Cavaliers to lead the Golden State Warriors in free throw percentage for a season?
   Answer on page 198.

50. Which former member of the Warriors holds the Indiana Pacers' career record for best free throw percentage?
   Answer on page 198.

51. Through the 2018–19 season, there have been 16 players to record 10 steals in a game. One player has 11, which is the current single-game record. Do you know who it is?
   Answer on page 198.

52. Who holds the NBA single-season record for blocked shots per game?
Answer on page 199.

53. In one season with the Los Angeles Lakers, this player missed more free throws than Steve Nash did in his entire 18-year career. Who was it?
Answer on page 199.

54. Which player received the longest suspension in league history?
A. Ron Artest
B. Rasheed Wallace
C. J. R. Rider
D. Bill Laimbeer
Answer on page 199.

55. Which NBA player was suspended for 68 games in 1997, the second-longest suspension in league history?
Answer on page 199.

56. Which NBA team holds the record for consecutive games lost?
Answer on page 199.

57. What is the longest game in NBA history (1946–present)?
Answer on page 199.

58. Which NBA team holds the record for most rebounds during a single game?
Answer on page 199.

59. Which player became the first in NBA history to record at least 1,000 assists in a single season?
Answer on page 199.

60. Since the player above recorded 1,000 assists in a season, only two other players have accomplished this feat. Can you name them? In addition, one player did so in multiple years. Do you know how many?
Answer on page 200.

61. Who is the oldest player to appear in an NBA game?
Answer on page 200.

62. Which team averaged the fewest points for a season in NBA history?
Answer on page 200.

63. Which team holds the record for most consecutive games with less than 100 points?
A. 1999–2000 Chicago Bulls
B. 1973–74 Detroit Pistons
C. 2001–02 Miami Heat
D. 1997–98 Cleveland Cavaliers
Answer on page 200.

64. Who holds the record for most consecutive free throws made by an NBA player?
A. Mark Price
B. Sherman Douglas
C. Michael Williams
D. Jeff Cook
Answer on page 200.

65. Who is the youngest player to score 50 points in a game?
A. Allen Iverson
B. Rick Barry
C. Brandon Jennings
D. LeBron James
Answer on page 200.

66. Who is the youngest player to score more than 50 points in a game?
A. Brandon Jennings
B. Rick Barry
C. Allen Iverson
D. LeBron James
Answer on page 200.

67. Who is the WNBA's all-time leader in career games played at the end of the 2018 season?
Answer on page 200.

68. Which future Hall of Famer led the league in field goal percentage 10 times?
A. Tim Duncan
B. Michael Jordan
C. Shaquille O'Neal
D. Kobe Bryant
Answer on page 200.

69. Which Hall of Fame player became the first in NBA history to lead the league in scoring and steals in the same season?
A. Bob Cousy
B. Michael Jordan
C. John Stockton
D. Walt Frazier
Answer on page 201.

70. Since becoming a recorded stat in 1973–74, who is the only player to record more than 400 blocks for a single season?
Answer on page 201.

RECORDS

ANSWERS

1. That would be George Yardley, who scored 2,001 points during the 1957–58 season as a member of the Detroit Pistons.

2. Neil Johnston in 1954–55 and Wilt Chamberlain from 1959–60 to 1962–63 and 1965–66.

3. Nate Thurmond of the Chicago Bulls, who had 22 points, 14 rebounds, 13 assists, and 12 blocked shots in a 120–115 win over the Atlanta Hawks at Chicago Stadium. The 33-year-old Thurmond was playing in his team's first game of the season.

4. On February 18, 1986, Alvin Robertson put up 20 points, 11 rebounds, 10 assists, and 10 steals as a member of the San Antonio Spurs in a win over the Phoenix Suns; on March 29, 1990, Hakeem Olajuwon put up 18 points, 16 rebounds, 10 assists, and 11 blocks as a member of the Houston Rockets in a loss to the Milwaukee Bucks; on February 17, 1994, David Robinson put up 34 points, 10 rebounds, 10 assists, and 10 blocks as a member of the Spurs in a loss to the Detroit Pistons.

5. That would be Russell Westbrook, who on March 22, 2017, against the Philadelphia 76ers, logged 18 points, 14 assists, and 11 rebounds in just 28 minutes on the floor. He also went 6-for-6 from the field, becoming only the sixth player to ever accomplish that feat.

6. That would be Wilt Chamberlain (three times), Wes Unseld, Draymond Green (twice), Bo Outlaw, and Nikola Jokić. In addition, Jokić is the only player to record a triple-double while shooting 1.000 from the floor and scoring more than 30 points.

7. Kareem Abdul-Jabbar, who accomplished this feat from 1973 through 1981. (B)

8. Jerry West of the Los Angeles Lakers recorded 10 steals against the Seattle SuperSonics on December 7, 1973. (A)

9. They would be John Lucas of the San Antonio Spurs, who did so against the Denver Nuggets on April 15, 1984, and Jeff Blake of the Portland Trail Blazers, who did so against the Los Angeles Clippers on February 22, 2009.

10. Kevin Love with 53 while as a member of the Minnesota Timberwolves during the 2010–11 season.

11. On December 29, 1997, Bubba Wells of the Dallas Mavericks fouled out in just three minutes against the Chicago Bulls.

12. That unflattering record is held by Joe Fulks of the Philadelphia Warriors, who missed 38 shots against the St. Louis Bombers on March 30, 1948. (C)

13. Dallas Maverick star Dirk Nowitzki made 24 free throws without a miss against the Oklahoma City Thunder on May 17, 2011.

14. Two of the greatest centers of all time: Wilt Chamberlain and Bill Russell. They also hold 24 of the top 25 spots.

15. Nate Thurmond of the San Francisco Warriors, who had 42 boards against the Detroit Pistons on November 9, 1965.

16. It's Wilt Chamberlain again, with 47.24 MPG.

17. That would be Robert Parish, who had a career scoring average of 14.5 PPG.

18. Rick Barry with the University of Miami; Oakland Oaks of the ABA; and San Francisco Warriors of the NBA.
NCAA: 1964–65, 37.4 PPG for the University of Miami
NBA: 1966–67, 35.6 PPG for the San Francisco Warriors
ABA: 1968–69, 34.0 PPG for the Oakland Oaks

19. With 4,657 personal fouls—79 more than Karl Malone—Kareem Abdul-Jabbar has the most in league history. (D)

20. Bill Russell won two championships as the player-coach of the Boston Celtics (1967–68 and 1968–69) after taking over the head coaching duties from Red Auerbach after the 1965–66 season—making Russell the league's first African American coach as well. (C)

21. False. Gheorghe Mureşan topped Bol by measuring in at 7-foot-7 and 5/8. Mureşan played for the Washington Bullets/Wizards from 1993 to 1998, then with the New Jersey Nets during the 1999–2000 season.

22. Not only does she have the highest points per game average for a single season, but also the second-highest. That would be Phoenix Mercury guard Diana Taurasi, who averaged 25.3 PPG during the 2006 WNBA season. (A)

23. Averaging 8.6 assists per game for the 2018 season, Chicago Sky guard Courtney Vandersloot has the highest average by any player in WNBA history. She is also second on the list with 8.1 APG during the 2017 season.

24. That would be Sacramento Monarchs guard Ticha Penicheiro, who averaged 8.0 assists per game during the 2002 season.

25. Trick question, as there are *two* correct answers! In the 2017 season, Connecticut Sun forward Jonquel Jones averaged 11.9 rebounds per game to set the highest league average. However, the following season, Minnesota Lynx center Sylvia Fowles matched that with 11.9. If you want to know who had the most in those seasons, that would be Fowles, who had 404 compared to Jones's 403. (A and B)

26. You would think it'd have been Kobe Bryant or Reggie Miller, but you would be wrong. Bryant had 17, while Miller had 23. J. J. Redick has 25, but is 22 behind the all-time leader. Yes, veteran Jamal Crawford has made 47 four-point plays during his career. (C)

27. With 8,549 points (and counting), Diana Taurasi is the all-time leading scorer in WNBA history. (C)

28. Over a 16-year career (and counting), Seattle Storm guard Sue Bird has the most dimes in league history with 2,831. (B)

29. With 3,356—40 more than Tamika Catchings—Rebekkah Brunson has the most rebounds in WNBA history. The five-time All-Star and 15-year veteran (and counting), Brunson has played with the Sacramento Monarchs (2004–09) and Minnesota Lynx (2010–present). Fun fact: She is also the only player in the WNBA to have won five championships. (D)

30. The only player with more than 800 career steals, Tamika Catchings blows everyone out of the water with a record 1,074. The second-closest, Ticha Penicheiro, has 764. (D)

31. With 877, center Margo Dydek has the most career blocks in WNBA history, collecting them while with the Utah Starzz (1998–2002), Sacramento Monarchs (2003–04), Connecticut Sun (2006–07), and Los Angeles Sparks (2008). (B)

32. George Yardley. The Detroit Falcons guard/forward scored 2,001 points during the 1957–58 season.

33. With 1,293 over 11 seasons in Philly, Julius Erving is the all-time blocks leader in 76ers history. (C)

34. Rookie guard Kevin Edwards averaged a team-best 13.8 points for the 15–67 Miami Heat. (B)

35. The Round Mound of Rebound, Philadelphia 76ers forward Charles Barkley averaged a league-best 14.6 rebounds during the 1986–87 season. Barkley was listed anywhere from 6-foot-4 3/4 to 6-foot-6 throughout his career. But even 6-foot-6 would make him the shortest to have led the league in rebounding for a season.

36. Alex English scored 21,645 points with the Denver Nuggets from 1979 to 1990. (A)

37. Did we throw you off by adding Vancouver? Well, while the Grizzlies moved from Canada to Tennessee for the 2001–02 season, Marc Gasol—who only played with the team in Memphis—scored 11,684 points with the Grizzlies from 2008 to 2019. (C)

38. Robert Parish grabbed 11,051 boards with the Celtics, from 1980 to 1994. (C)

39. Playing with the Kings from 1974 to 1981, Scott Wedman scored 9,002 points during the team's time in Kansas City. (D)

40. Devin Booker collected back-to-back 50-point games, doing so on March 25, 2019 (a 50-point performance in a loss to the Washington Wizards) and on March 27, 2019 (a 59-point performance in a loss to the Utah Jazz), becoming the youngest player to ever accomplish this feat, at 20 years and 146/148 days old. (B)

41. At 34 years and 92 days, Bernard King is the oldest player to score 50 points in a game, doing so in a loss to the Utah Jazz on March 6, 1991, while as a member of the Washington Bullets. (C)

42. At 38 years and 315 days, Michael Jordan is the oldest player to score more than 50 points in a game, scoring 51 in a win over the Golden State Warriors on November 14, 2009, while as a member of the Washington Wizards. (A)

43. Not only do they have the third-highest scoring total, but the fourth, fifth, seventh, *and* eleventh! Oh, as well as the top spot. That's right, Wilt Chamberlain scored 78 points in a game—the third most all time—on December 8, 1961, but has also scored 73 (twice), 72, and 70 points in a single game.

44. Charlie Scott, who averaged 34.6 points for the Virginia Squires in 1971–72. (C)

45. Zydrunas Ilgauskas, with 10,616 points in a Cavaliers uniform.

46. Hal Greer, with 21,586 points for the Syracuse Nats/Philadelphia 76ers.

47. Luol Deng, who scored 10,286 points as a member of the Chicago Bulls from 2004 to 2014. Former Utah Jazz coach Jerry Sloan rounds out the top five at 10,233 points.

48. Rik Smits, who finished with 12,871 points during a 12-year career with Indiana—the only franchise for which he ever played.

49. Mark Price, who shot .906 from the line for the Golden State Warriors in 1996–97.

50. Chris Mullin, who shot .912 from the line in his two seasons with the Pacers (1998–99 and 1999–2000). He was a .865 shooter from the charity stripe for his 16-year career.

51. On April 3, 1999, New Jersey Nets guard Kendall Gill recorded 11 steals (to go along with 15 points and 10 rebounds) against the Miami Heat. The Nets would win the game, 88–77, which was only their seventh of the season.

52. Mark Eaton, who swatted 5.56 shots per game for the Utah Jazz in 1984–85. Eaton led the league in blocks per game a total of four times. The only other players to do that since the league started keeping the stat in 1973–74? Kareem Abdul-Jabbar and Marcus Camby.

53. Dwight Howard, who missed 366 shots from the line during his 2012–13 season with the Los Angeles Lakers. In 18 NBA seasons, Nash only missed 324 overall.

54. During the 2004 Pistons-Pacers brawl, a.k.a. the "Malice at The Palace," Pacers forward Ron Artest (now known as Metta World Peace) charged the stands and threw punches at fans after a fan threw a cup at him. Artest was suspended for 73 games, along with 13 playoff games. It cost him $7 million in salary. (A)

55. Latrell Sprewell of the Golden State Warriors, who attacked and choked his Warriors coach, P. J. Carlesimo, during a practice on December 1, 1997. Sprewell choked Carlesimo for 15 seconds before teammates pulled him away. He would next play for the New York Knicks after being traded as a result of the incident.

56. The 2010–11 Cleveland Cavaliers, who dropped 26 in a row en route to a 19–63 record for the season. This was, of course, the season *after* LeBron James left the franchise for the Miami Heat in free agency.

57. The Indianapolis Olympians and the Rochester Royals played a six-overtime game on January 6, 1951. Indianapolis survived with a 75–73 victory.

58. The Boston Celtics, who hauled in 109 boards on December 24, 1960, against the Detroit Pistons. Bill Russell pulled in 29 while Sam Jones added 16.

59. Kevin Porter of the Detroit Pistons, who passed for 1,099 assists during the 1978–79 season.

60. The other two players, aside from Kevin Porter, to dish 1,000 assists in a single season were Isiah Thomas and John Stockton. Thomas did so during the 1984–85 season, but Stockton did so *seven* times (1987–1992, 1993–95).

61. Nat Hickey of the Providence Steamrollers, who appeared in two games during the 1947–48 season, the second of which at 45 years and 363 days old.

62. The 1998–99 Chicago Bulls scored a meager 81.90 points per game. Not surprisingly, that was the season after Michael Jordan retired and Scottie Pippen was traded to the Houston Rockets.

63. The 2001–02 Miami Heat went 35 consecutive games without reaching 100 points. (C)

64. Michael Williams of the Minnesota Timberwolves, with 97 straight free throws made, from March 24, 1993, through November 9, 1993. (C)

65. At 21 years and 309 days, Allen Iverson is the youngest player to score 50 points in a game, doing so in a loss to the Clevland Cavaliers on April 12, 1997, while as a member of the Philadelphia 76ers. (A)

66. At 20 years and 52 days, Brandon Jennings is the youngest player to score more than 50 points in a game, scoring 55 in a win over the Golden State Warriors on November 14, 2009, as a member of the Milwaukee Bucks. (A)

67. Sue Bird has played in the most games in WNBA history (508).

68. Remember, we said field goal percentage, not free throw percentage. That's right, Shaquille O'Neal led the league in field goal percentage a whopping 10 times, while Wilt Chamberlain *only* led the league nine times.

69. Averaging 35.0 points and 3.2 steals during the 1987–88 season, Michael Jordan became the first player to lead the lead in both categories for a single season. (B)

70. In the 1984–85 season, Utah Jazz center Mark Eaton blocked 456 shots. He is currently the only player in NBA history to have blocked 400 shots in a single season (though Artis Gilmore blocked 422 during the 1971–72 ABA season).

QUESTIONS

In basketball, it is considered the ultimate honor, a way to be remembered forever and have your legacy on display for all the world to see. And most everyone who has played the sport has at one time or another dreamed about making it all the way to the hall of fame.

For hoops, the official name is the Naismith Memorial Basketball Hall of Fame. It is named after the game's inventor, Dr. James Naismith, and located in Springfield, Massachusetts, the site of where the first game was played.

Naismith was an instructor and teacher at YMCA in Springfield, and tried to find a sport for his class to play in the cold of winter. So he hung a couple of peach baskets in 1891 and everyone who loves the game today will tell you that is when the world changed for the better.

The hall of fame isn't about just the men and women who played or coached. It also honors contributors and media members, and on occasion, people who have done a little of everything.

The following questions are on those whose basketball dreams have been realized and whose hoops memories will dribble on forever.

1. What year did the Naismith Memorial Basketball Hall of Fame open?
   Answer on page 211.

2. Who was the first international player to be inducted into the Hall of Fame?
   Answer on page 211.

3. Which Hall of Famer has the lowest free throw percentage for their career?
A. Shaquille O'Neal
B. Bill Russell
C. Dennis Rodman
D. Wilt Chamberlain
Answer on page 211.

4. Which Hall of Famer has the highest free throw percentage for their career?
A. Ray Allen
B. Reggie Miller
C. Steve Nash
D. Larry Bird
Answer on page 211.

5. Match the Hall of Famer to their college:

1. Larry Bird	A.	Southern Illinois
2. Manute Bol	B.	San Francisco
3. Steve Nash	C.	Eastern Michigan
4. Scottie Pippen	D.	DePaul
5. George Mikan	E.	Indiana State
6. Robert Parish	F.	Santa Clara
7. George Gervin	G.	Central Arkansas
8. Earl Monroe	H.	Bridgeport
9. Walt Frazier	I.	Winston-Salem State
10. Bill Russell	J.	Centenary

Answer on page 211.

6. Which Hall of Famer has the most career playoff points without winning a championship?
A. Elgin Baylor
B. Karl Malone
C. Charles Barkley
D. Patrick Ewing
Answer on page 211.

7. Who are the only two players since the Lottery Era (starting in 1985) to make the Hall of Fame after being picked in the second round?
Answer on page 211.

8. Which player was the latest pick in a draft to make the Hall of Fame?
Answer on page 212.

9. Since the Lottery Era (and as of 2019), how many No. 1 overall picks have made the Hall of Fame?
Answer on page 212.

10. Which four individuals have been inducted into the Hall of Fame as both a player and coach?
A. Lenny Wilkens, John Wooden, Tom Heinsohn, Larry Brown
B. Lenny Wilkens, John Wooden, Tom Heinsohn, Bill Sharman
C. Bob Cousy, John Wooden, Tom Heinsohn, John McLendon
D. K. C. Jones, Lenny Wilkens, Bill Sharmon, Bill Russell
Answer on page 212.

11. Which individual has been inducted into the Hall of Fame as both a coach and contributor?
A. Clair Bee
B. Chuck Daly
C. John McLendon
D. Jim Boeheim
Answer on page 212.

12. Which Hall of Famer holds the league record for leading the NBA in free throw percentage seven times?
Answer on page 212.

13. Who is the shortest NBA player inducted into the Hall of Fame?
Answer on page 212.

14. Name the only three players 7-foot-3 or taller to be inducted into the Hall of Fame.
Answer on page 212.

15. What made the induction classes of 1965, 1968, and 2007 particularly unique?
Answer on page 212.

16. Which team has had the most Hall of Fame players on its roster?
Answer on page 212.

17. Which two NBA players share the honor of winning the most championship rings (seven) *without* being members of the Hall of Fame?
Answer on page 213.

18. Which Hall of Fame Celtic did *not* begin his career in Boston?
A. Larry Bird
B. Kevin McHale
C. Robert Parish
D. Danny Ainge
Answer on page 213.

19. Name the only player to be a member of both the Basketball and Baseball Halls of Fame.
Answer on page 213.

20. Which team, enshrined into the Hall of Fame in 2002, played the first-ever night game in the history of Wrigley Field?
Answer on page 213.

21. Which Hall of Fame guard came out of tiny McNeese State, yet went on to play 14 seasons in the NBA, totaling 16,401 points, 1,388 steals, and helping his team to a pair of championships?
Answer on page 213.

22. In which city was Hall of Famer Dominique Wilkins born?
A. Atlanta, Georgia
B. Baltimore, Maryland
C. London, England
D. Paris, France
Answer on page 213.

23. Which Hall of Famer was named Defensive Player of the Year with three different franchises?
A. Shaquille O'Neal
B. Wilt Chamberlain
C. Dikembe Mutombo
D. Dennis Rodman
Answer on page 213.

24. Which Hall of Fame player served as mayor of Detroit, Michigan, from 2009 to 2013?
A. Kevin Johnson
B. Dave Bing
C. Joe Dumars
D. David Robinson
Answer on page 213.

25. Which of these Hall of Famers also has a relative in the Hall?
A. Reggie Miller
B. Jerry West
C. Walt Frazier
D. Oscar Robertson
Answer on page 213.

26. Which of these Hall of Famers played for five teams during his career?
A. Wilt Chamberlain
B. Karl Malone
C. Dominique Wilkins
D. Dennis Rodman
Answer on page 214.

27. Which of these Los Angeles Lakers Hall of Famers never played on a team that defeated the Boston Celtics in the NBA Finals?

A. Jamaal Wilkes

B. Magic Johnson

C. Jerry West

D. Bob McAdoo

Answer on page 214.

28. Which of these Hall of Famers played on the original "Dream Team" in the 1992 Summer Olympics in Barcelona?

A. Shaquille O'Neal

B. Clyde Drexler

C. Joe Dumars

D. Isiah Thomas

Answer on page 214.

29. The Toronto Raptors drafted which Hall of Famer in 1997?

A. Alonzo Mourning

B. Vince Carter

C. Tracy McGrady

D. Shaquille O'Neal

Answer on page 214.

30. Which Hall of Famer played for four consecutive WNBA championship squads?

A. Cheryl Miller

B. Rebecca Lobo

C. Lisa Leslie

D. Sheryl Swoopes

Answer on page 214.

31. Which of these Hall of Famers was inducted posthumously?
A. Pete Maravich
B. Connie Hawkins
C. Dražen Petrović
D. Moses Malone
Answer on page 214.

32. Which Hall of Famer player appeared in the *least* amount of games for his career?
Answer on page 214.

HALL OF FAME

ANSWERS

1. The Naismith Memorial Basketball Hall of Fame opened on February 17, 1968.

2. Sergei Belov of the Soviet national team in 1992.

3. If you want to make it to the HOF, you must hit your free throws! Amazingly, no HOFer has shot less than 50 percent from the charity stripe, but Wilt Chamberlain just eeked out Shaquille O'Neal for the lowest, .511 to .527. (D)

4. Oh, Canada! Steve Nash has the highest free throw percentage for a career of any Hall of Famer with .904, just beating out the Granny-style king, Rick Barry (.900). (C)

5. 1-E, 2-H, 3-F, 4-G, 5-D, 6-J, 7-C, 8-I, 9-A, 10-B

6. Playing in 193 playoff games, Karl Malone scored 4,761 points without ever winning a championship. He currently ranks No. 7 on the all-time playoff scoring list. (B)

7. Dennis Rodman was drafted in the second round (27th overall) in the 1986 draft, and was inducted into the Hall of Fame in 2011; Dino Radja was drafted in the second round (40th overall) in the 1989 draft, and was inducted into the Hall of Fame in 2018.

8. Šarūnas Marčiulionis was drafted in the sixth round (127th overall) in the 1987 draft, and was inducted into the Hall of Fame in 2014.

9. Five players taken first overall in the Lottery Era have been inducted in the Hall of Fame:
Patrick Ewing, 1985
David Robinson, 1987
Shaquille O'Neal, 1992
Allen Iverson, 1996
Yao Ming, 2002

10. Lenny Wilkens, John Wooden, Tom Heinsohn, Bill Sharman (B)

11. John McLendon compiled more than 400 college career wins with Tennessee State A&I University and North Carolina College from 1941 to 1952 and coached the ABL's Cleveland Pipers, owned by George Steinbrenner, during their lone season of 1961–62. (C)

12. Hall of Famer Bill Sharman led the league seven times, doing so from 1952–53 to 1956–57 as well as in 1958–59 and 1960–61. The 1960–61 season was the last of his career, and he had a .921 free throw percentage for the season, at age 34.

13. Longtime Houston Rockets guard Calvin Murphy, who stands 5-foot-9, is the shortest member of the Hall of Fame, and was inducted in 1993.

14. Ralph Sampson (7-foot-4), Arvydas Sabonis (7-foot-3), and Yao Ming (7-foot-6).

15. Those were the only three times a class was inducted without honoring a player.

16. The Boston Celtics, with 25.

17. Jim Loscutoff of the Boston Celtics and Robert Horry, who played for multiple teams, the latter winning three titles with the Los Angeles Lakers and two each with the Houston Rockets and San Antonio Spurs.

18. Starting his career with the Golden State Warriors, "The Chief" Robert Parish was the only one to not join the league as a member of the Boston Celtics. (C)

19. Cumberland Posey Jr., who was elected into the Basketball Hall of Fame in 2016. Ten years earlier, in 2006, he was elected to the Baseball Hall of Fame.

20. That would be the Harlem Globetrotters. The magicians of round-ball played a game under portable lights at the venerable ballpark on August 21, 1954, defeating George Mikan's U.S. Stars, 57–51.

21. Joe Dumars of the Detroit Pistons, who won back-to-back NBA titles in 1989 and 1990.

22. On January 12, 1960, Dominique Wilkins was born in Paris, France. With his father stationed in Paris as an airman in the US Air Force, Dominique and his family later moved to Dallas and then Baltimore, before settling in Washington, North Carolina. (D)

23. Winning the award with the Denver Nuggets (1994–95), Atlanta Hawks (1996–97 and 1997–98), and the Philadelphia 76ers (2000–01), Dikembe Mutombo is the only Hall of Fame player to win the Defensive POY Award with three different teams. (C)

24. After a 12-year Hall of Fame career (nine of them with the Pistons), Dave Bing would serve one term as the mayor of Detroit. (B)

25. Reggie Miller, along with his sister Cheryl (who was inducted seventeen years before her brother), are both members of the Naismith Memorial Basketball Hall of Fame. (A)

26. Of the players listed, Dominique Wilkins is the only to have played for five different teams. Joining the league as an Atlanta Hawk—where he played for 12 seasons—he would go on to play for the Los Angeles Clippers, Boston Celtics, San Antonio Spurs, and Orlando Magic. In addition, he also spent seasons playing ball in Greece and Italy. (C)

27. Going 0–6 against the Celtics, Jerry West was never able to defeat Boston in the NBA Finals. (C)

28. Of the names mentioned, Clyde Drexler was the only member of the "Dream Team." (B)

29. With the ninth overall pick in the 1997 draft, taken straight from high school, the Toronto Raptors selected Tracy McGrady. He would only play three seasons of his 15-year career in Canada. (C)

30. Hall of Famer Sheryl Swoopes won the WNBA Finals four times as a member of the Houston Comets (1997–2000). (D)

31. On June 7, 1993, Dražen Petrović lost his life in a fatal car accident. While he only played four years in the league, he won a bronze and two silver medals in the Olympics with Yugoslavia (1984, 1988, and 1992, respectively). Petrović was inducted into the Hall of Fame in 2002, and his No. 3 was retired by the Nets. In addition, Hall of Famer Reggie Miller—one of the greatest shooters in NBA history—once called Dražen "the best three-point shooter I've ever seen." (C)

32. Though his career started a decade before the 1946–47 inaugural season, Buddy Jeannette appeared in only 139 games. It is the least of any player who was inducted in the HOF (as a player).

Postgame

If you've reached it this far, congratulations. You are now officially an expert. And if not, hopefully you know more about basketball than before you started. Hopefully you had a chance to learn more about the game you love, its rich (and often undertold) history, its record holders, and that the NBA isn't the only show in town.

Along with those in the NBA, the game has been shaped by women and amateurs, people from all walks of life, all sizes and from all over the world. Some of the records here will be broken soon. Some will live on forever. Others are "firsts" that can only be accomplished once. But there are undoubtedly more firsts to come. At least, there are as long as their remains someone who grabs a ball, finds a basket, and falls in love with the game.

But as you hopefully realized within these pages, while the players and coaches get all the glory, basketball is about more than just the men and women in uniform or roaming the sidelines. These days, it takes much more to make the sport work—from team owners to athletic directors to the medical staff to the dreaded referees

Oh, and let's not forget about those amazing sportswriters.

Mostly, though, basketball is able to reach new heights because of those who are willing to watch it and support it. It survives and flourishes because of you, the fan. Without you, basketball may never have advanced beyond the stage of a kid in the driveway lofting up shots.

It really is true: Those who love the game make the game something special. They keep the ball bouncing and have been the primary reason basketball has become big business.

If you're reading this, then you belong to that special club, and this book is for you.

Acknowledgments

This book would not have existed without the vision and support of Jason Katzman, who guided me through the project and proved to be the Scottie Pippen of editors.

Thanks also to my amazing wife, Katie, who serves as my agent and business manager, and the person who helped control the chaos to make sure I had time to research and write. She was as important to this book getting done as I was.

Also offering an inordinate amount of inspiration were some of those who make a living in basketball and have occasionally gone out of their way to make me feel like a major part of it: Spencer Haywood, Larry Bird, Artis Gilmore, Robert Reid, Mark Price, Eric Musselman, Austin Carr, and Campy Russell, who I am blessed to call a friend.

Finally, to all of those who have played a role in me becoming a writer and completing this project, or just being a great friend: Jeff Phelps, Brian Twiddy, Matt Loede, and my late father, Paul Amico, who handed down his love of the game. This book is partially dedicated to his memory.